COMPUTING MADE

GW00717047

AT ONLY £7.99 •   K

BESTSELLER
Works for Windows 3.1 (Version 3)
P. K. McBride
0 7506 2065 X   1994

Lotus 1-2-3 (2.4 DOS Version)
Ian Robertson
0 7506 2066 8   1994

WordPerfect (DOS 6.0)
Stephen Copestake
0 7506 2068 4   1994

BESTSELLER
MS DOS (Up To Version 6.22)
Ian Sinclair
0 7506 2069 2   1994

BESTSELLER
Excel For Windows 3.1 (Version 5)
Stephen Morris
0 7506 2070 6   1994

BESTSELLER
Word For Windows 3.1 (Version 6)
Keith Brindley
0 7506 2071 4   1994

BESTSELLER
Windows 3.1
P. K. McBride
0 7506 2072 2   1994

BESTSELLER
Windows 95
P. K. McBride
0 7506 2306 3   1995

Lotus 1-2-3 for Windows 3.1 (Version 5)
Stephen Morris
0 7506 2307 1   1995

BESTSELLER
Access For Windows 3.1 (Version 2)
Moira Stephen
0 7506 2309 8   1995

BESTSELLER
Internet for Windows 3.1
P. K. McBride
0 7506 2311 X   1995

Pageplus for Windows 3.1 (Version 3)
Ian Sinclair
0 7506 2312 8   1995

Hard Drives
Ian Sinclair
0 7506 2313 6   1995

BESTSELLER
Multimedia for Windows 3.1
Simon Collin
0 7506 2314 4   1995

Powerpoint for Windows 3.1 (Version 4.0)
Moira Stephen
0 7506 2420 5   1995

Office 95
P. K. McBride
0 7506 2625 9   1995

Word Pro for Windows 3.1 (Version 4.0)
Moira Stephen
0 7506 2626 7   1995

BESTSELLER
Word for Windows 95 (Version 7)
Keith Brindley
0 7506 2815 4   1996

BESTSELLER
Excel for Windows 95 (Version 7)
Stephen Morris
0 7506 2816 2   1996

Powerpoint for Windows 95 (Version 7)
Moira Stephen
0 7506 2817 0   1996

BESTSELLER
Access for Windows 95 (Version 7)
Moira Stephen
0 7506 2818 9   1996

BESTSELLER
Internet for Windows 95
P. K. McBride
0 7506 2835 9   1996

Internet Resources
P. K. McBride
0 7506 2836 7   1996

Microsoft Networking
P. K. McBride
0 7506 2837 5   1996

Designing Internet Home Pages
Lilian Hobbs
0 7506 2941 X   1996

BESTSELLER
Works for Windows 95 (Version 4.0)
P. K. McBride
0 7506 3396 4   1996

NEW
Windows NT (Version 4.0)
Lilian Hobbs
0 7506 3511 8   1997

NEW
Compuserve
Keith Brindley
0 7506 3512 6   1997

NEW
Microsoft Internet Explorer
Sam Kennington
0 7506 3513 4   1997

NEW
Netscape Navigator
Sam Kennington
0 7506 3514 2   1997

NEW
Searching The Internet
Sam Kennington
0 7506 3794 3   1997

NEW
The Internet for Windows 3.1 (Second Edition)
P. K. McBride
0 7506 3795 1   1997

NEW
The Internet for Windows 95 (Second Edition)
P. K. McBride
0 7506 3846 X   1997

NEW
Office 97 for Windows
P. K. McBride
0 7506 3798 6   1997

NEW
Powerpoint 97 For Windows
Moira Stephen
0 7506 3799 4   1997

NEW
Access 97 For Windows
Moira Stephen
0 7506 3800 1   1997

NEW
Word 97 For Windows
Keith Brindley
0 7506 3801 X   1997

NEW
Excel 97 For Windows
Stephen Morris
0 7506 3802 8   1997

Windows NT
Made Simple

Lilian Hobbs

MADE SIMPLE
BOOKS

Made Simple
An imprint of Butterworth-Heinemann
Linacre House, Jordan Hill, Oxford OX2 8DP
A division of Reed Educational and Professional Publishing Ltd

↺ A member of the Reed Elsevier plc group

OXFORD   BOSTON   JOHANNESBURG
MELBOURNE   NEW DELHI   SINGAPORE

First published 1997
Reprinted 1997

British Library Cataloguing in Publication Data
A catalogue record for this book is available from the British Library

ISBN 0 7506 3511 8

Typeset by Lilian Hobbs, Southampton
Archtype, Bash Casual, Cotswold and Gravity fonts from Advanced Graphics Ltd
Icons designed by Sarah Ward © 1994
Printed and bound in Great Britain by Scotprint, Musselburgh, Scotland

Contents

Preface

Today, the vast majority of small computers in the world are running one of the versions of Windows from Microsoft. Windows has been evolving over the years, and the most sophisticated version yet released is Windows NT V4.

The first chapter introduces you to Windows NT and positions it in relation to Windows 95 and Windows for Workgroups.

Chapters 2 and 3, guide you through setting up an NT system. Thankfully, due to its graphical interfaces, these steps are easy to follow – they are also likely to be repeated at various times in the future.

Chapter 4 explains how to create and manage a username and password. Chapters 5 and 6 describe how to manage printers and perform important tasks like backing up the files on the computer.

Most NT computers will be attached to a network and Chapters 7 and 8 will introduce you to these concepts and how to attach your computer to the network.

Finally, no book today is complete without a chapter on the Internet and Chapter 9 describes how to turn your computer into a World Wide Web site.

It is assumed that readers of this book have a basic understanding of Windows software concepts from using products like Windows for Workgroups or Windows 95. If you are not familiar with these products then good references are *Windows Made Simple* and *Windows 95 Made Simple*.

1 Overview

The Windows story

When historians look back at how computers have evolved into almost a household item, they should all say that a significant reason for their success was Windows from Microsoft.

When the first personal computers appeared, they were primitive machines that could only really be used by computer people. All that began to change with the introduction of **MS-DOS** from Microsoft which for the first time allowed non-computer literate users the chance to control a computer.

MS-DOS was a very popular **operating system**. At one time it was estimated that there were in excess of 100 million copies installed on computers around the globe. MS-DOS had many limitations, among them was the fact that it wasn't very friendly to use.

Commands were given to the computer from the keyboard, if you didn't know the command, then you couldn't tell the computer what to do unless you read the manual. Now for computer types this is not a problem, but for us ordinary folk this is just too much to ask!

The command DIRECTORY is not recognised

The command is DIR to see the contents of the directory

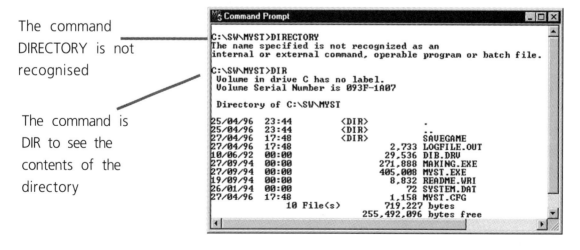

2

Jargon

GUI stands for Graphical User Interface. It is a way of communicating with a computer using pictures and a mouse rather than commands.

Microsoft Windows is a GUI-based operating system from Microsoft.

Icon is a graphical picture that represents an action e.g. Save file to disk. When the mouse is clicked over the icon, the action is performed.

Computer companies, aware that they had to change the method of communicating with the user, introduced the **GUI**. Instead of typing commands like DIR to see the files in a directory, the user was presented with a picture of the information and using the mouse, could point to commands which told the computer what to do.

The mouse was a revolutionary step forward in human communication with the computer. Several attempts were made at creating GUI operating systems, but the one that has proved to be the most popular is Windows from Microsoft.

When using a GUI interface, the commands are either visible from a strip menu, an **icon** or you can click with the mouse over the name of an object to start an action. e.g. to see the contents of the directory, click on its name in the directory list.

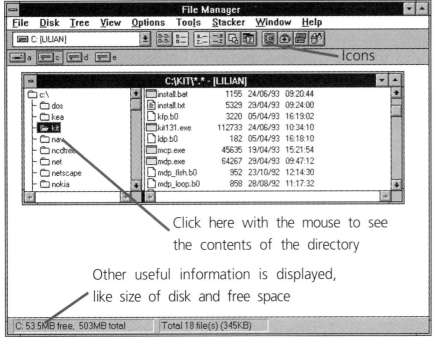

Microsoft Windows has become one of the world's best selling software products. Initially it was called Microsoft Windows and new versions 2 and 3 were released. The next version, 3.11, Windows for Workgroups, allowed a user to share their files and printers with other users.

Icons

Click here with the mouse to see the contents of the directory

Other useful information is displayed, like size of disk and free space

Introducing Windows 95

Windows was immensely popular, but its capabilities were limited. You could only perform one job at a time. Some people felt that the displays were still not easy for everyone to understand and PC users started looking towards a 32-bit operating system.

With more hype and marketing than a blockbuster film, Windows 95 appeared on the scene and has been as successful as its predecessors, despite having a totally new look and feel.

The background is called the **desktop** and icons can be placed on the desktop to quick start the tasks that you want to do.

You can place applications and documents here on the desktop

An application can be run by clicking on the icon

Jargon

32-bit Operating System – one designed to run on computers with a 32-bit chip.

Desktop – the background where documents and programs are placed. It shows you what is available and what you are working on.

Document – a text, graphic or data file.

Application – a program such as Explorer, Calculator or PageMaker 6.

Tip

Instead of trying to remember what you are working on, put the documents and files here on the desktop.

This is the Desktop

Why not NT

- ❏ More expensive than Windows 95.

- ❏ Very old hardware may not run NT.

- ❏ Some applications may not run on NT.

- ❏ System requirements are slightly higher than for Windows 95.

- ❏ NT 4.0 does not support Plug & Play.

Why not Windows 95

- ❏ Doesn't offer all the functionality of NT.

- ❏ Limited security.

Take note

Plug & Play means that when a new device such as a soundcard is added, the system automatically detects it and prompts you for any necessary information.

At first glance Windows 95 and Windows NT V4.0 look identical, so which one is the better?

Windows NT

Windows NT is the better choice for business or serious home users because it:

- ● Can perform multiple tasks at once, more efficiently than Windows 95.

- ● Provides more functionality than Windows 95.

- ● Is enabled as a Web Server (see page 124).

- ● Offers good security.

- ● Has the same interface as Windows 95 so it is easy to use.

Windows 95

Is the ideal choice for the home user if cost is of primary consideration, because it offers many of the features of Windows NT.

- ● Is much cheaper than Windows NT.

- ● Same interface as Windows NT.

- ● Offers limited multi-tasking.

- ● Is the easy way to upgrade from Windows 3.1 and Windows for Workgroups.

- ● Microsoft is committed to providing an upgrade path to Windows NT Workstation should you decide to upgrade to NT in the future.

What is Windows NT?

Microsoft Windows **NT** is an operating system which offers high performance, good security and the reliability that is demanded when used by a company to support its business.

So what is special about NT? Why have Microsoft put so much effort into this product?

- It supports **multi-tasking**. e.g. spell check a large document and create a presentation at the same time.

- Applications can be written to take advantage of **multi-threading**. e.g. computes the positions of objects in the sky while the user is entering some comet data.

- Security at the file level.

- In-built **networking**.

- Ready to be a **Web server**.

- Designed to support many users.

- Provides high performance.

- Robust operating system that will not fail easily.

This is not the first release of Windows NT – there have been several before – but this is the first one that uses the Windows 95 interface.

At first glance, Windows NT and 95 look identical, but when you delve underneath, you will start to see that they are quite different. Some of the differences are very subtle, like additional options available with a feature.

Most applications that were designed to run on MS-DOS, Windows or Windows 95 should run happily on NT.

Jargon

NT stands for New Technology.

Multi-tasking is the ability to execute more than one job at a time.

Multi-threading means that an application can perform multiple tasks at the same time.

Networking is when two or more computers are connected.

Web server is the application that allows you to turn your computer into a World Wide Web site.

Tip

With the software there is a book containing a list of all the computers that can run Windows **NT**. Check your machine is there.

If it isn't, try anyway.

The Platform

486, Pentium, RISC or Alpha processor

12 to 16Mb memory

CD-ROM

110Mb free disk space

VGA or better display

Mouse

At first glance it's difficult to tell if this is a Windows 95 or a Windows NT system, because Windows NT has the same look and feel as Windows 95. As soon as you click over the word **Start** and the menu is shown, the words *NT Workstation* will be displayed. There is the answer to the question.

If you are use to using Windows 95 then you will find moving to NT very easy. If not, then don't worry, all will become apparent very soon.

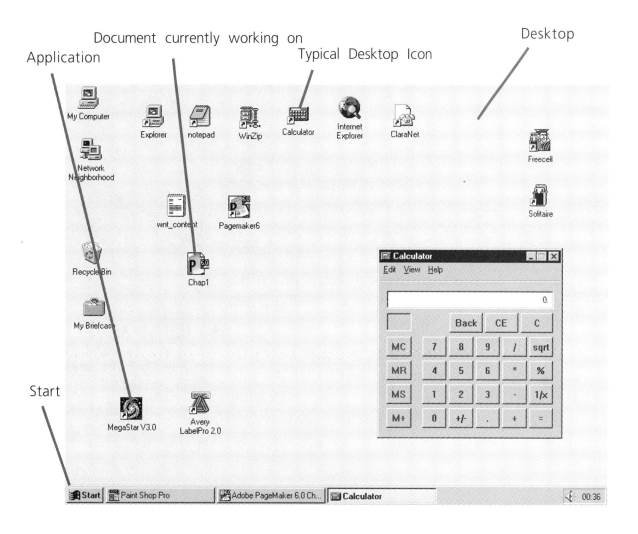

Preparing to install

Installing NT is quite straightforward but it is wise to do some preparation beforehand.

The first step is to take a backup of your system. Don't worry if you don't have a tape drive. Your backup could be as simple as copying the most important files to floppy disks or another hard disk, if you have one.

Windows NT is installed from the CD-ROM and the floppy disks. If you look at the CD you will see that it contains the installation files for several different platforms. e.g. the Alpha chip in Digital Equipment machines and I386 refers to computers with Intel chips.

Also included on the CD, you will find an on-line copy of the documentation which you will need because no manuals are provided.

Windows NT can be installed to run alongside systems like Windows 95. When the computer is switched on, you will be asked which system you want to run. If you install alongside another system like Windows 95, NT will be installed in another directory so there is no need to worry about overwriting your existing Windows 95 installation.

Another important check, is that your machine is up to the job of running Windows NT. In particular you will find that more memory will make things run faster.

A floppy disk is needed during the installation because this disk will become the Emergency Repair Disk (see page 39). This must be kept safe, preferably at another location, because if you ever have a problem with NT, you may need this disk to restore your system.

(see page 39)

Basic steps

1 Make sure that your system matches the Windows NT hardware requirements.

2 Backup your system or copy the important files to a disk or floppy disks.

3 Get a spare floppy disk which will be needed during the installation.

4 Decide whether you will use the FAT or NTFS file system.

Tip

If you already have a previous version of NT installed, don't forget to purchase the upgrade version, which will save you quite a bit of money.

Basic steps

5 If the computer is going to be connected to a network, obtain its network address and name.

6 Read the Start Here book section on Installation.

Tip

NT can be installed so that you can choose at boot time whether to run it or say Windows 95.

NT provides two file systems, FAT and NTFS. During installation you will be asked which one you want to use.

A disk formatted with NTFS can only be read by a system running NT. If you have computers running Windows 95 or Windows for Workgroups that need access to your NT system, then they must be formatted using the FAT system. See page 11 for more on the FAT and NTFS file systems.

If your computer is going to be connected to a network, then during the installation you will be asked for its network identity.

Finally read the Start Here book, supplied with the NT software, which is divided into two parts. The first section will tell you about the new features in NT V4.0. The second section should be read carefully because, it will explain all the installation steps.

Software to install on a Pentium

On-line Documentation

Contents of the Windows NT CDROM

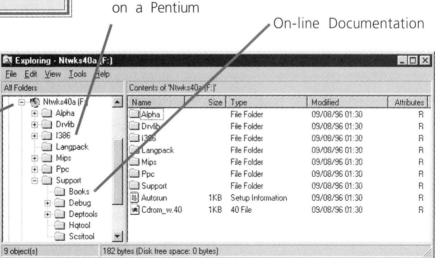

Is NT Workstation OK?

Two types of Windows NT are available:

● NT Server.

● NT Workstation.

So, just when you thought it was safe to get started, there is another decision to make. Which one should you choose? For the majority of home users, NT Workstation should be sufficient.

NT Server

● Unlimited **client connections**.

● Supports up to 32 **CPUs**.

● Up to 256 **remote access service** sessions.

● Optimised for server and background tasks.

● Other options such as Macintosh services and disk service.

NT Workstation

● A limit of 10 concurrent input sessions, but you can have as many sessions leaving your computer as you like.

● Supports only 2 **CPUs**. Home computers usually have 1 CPU.

● Only 1 **remote access service** session. This means that only one person can dial-in to you computer at a time.

Jargon

Client Connections refers to other users connecting to your computer.

CPU is the Central Processing Unit in the computer where the instructions are executed.

Remote access service allows another user to dial-in to your computer.

Take note

If you are a business user, carefully assess if Workstation will give you all the functionality and power that you need.

FAT or NTFS

FAT stands for File Allocation Table.

NTFS stands for NT File System.

Security on a file enables you to specify which users can access a file and what actions they can perform.

Partition is an area on a disk that behaves as a separate disk.

Striped sets are created from two or more disks, using exactly the same amount of space on each disk. Once created it appears as a single disk.

Volume sets are created, so that one or more partitions are merged together to look like a single disk. Useful when have a number of different size partitions that could be used to create one large disk.

While you are installing NT or whenever you add a new disk to your computer, you will be asked which file system you want to use. NT gives you the choice of:

- FAT
- NTFS

FAT

If you have used Windows 3.1 or Windows 95 you will be familiar with the FAT system. I won't bore you with the technical differences, but if you use the FAT system then you can:

- read/write to the disk from Windows 3.1, 95 and NT.
- name a file using up to 155 characters.
- run multiple operating systems from the disk e.g. Windows 95 and NT.

NTFS

Unless you want to share your disks with users of DOS or Windows, there are several advantages to using NTFS.

- name a file up to 255 characters.
- each file can have its own **security**.
- can create **striped** and **volume** sets using two or more disk.
- ability to create files larger than those allowed by FAT.
- the disk cannot be read by a computer running Windows 3.1 or Windows '95. This could be considered a security feature!

11

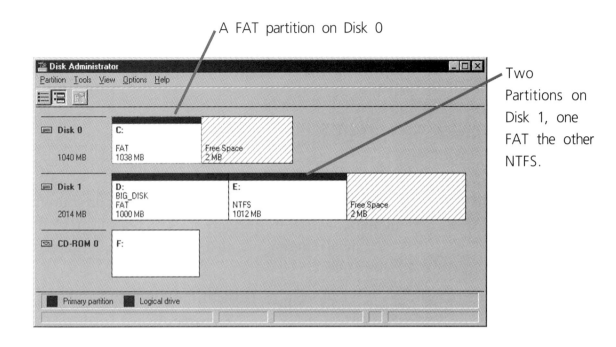

A FAT partition on Disk 0

Two Partitions on Disk 1, one FAT the other NTFS.

Stripe Disk

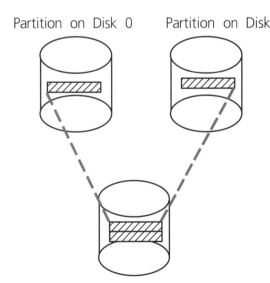

Partition on Disk 0   Partition on Disk 1

The logical Disk D uses the two partitions from Disks 0 and 1.

Volume Disk

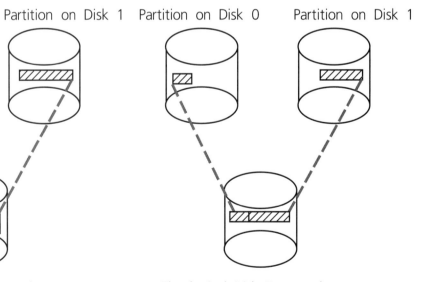

Partition on Disk 0   Partition on Disk 1

The logical Disk D uses the two partitions from Disks 0 and 1.

Basic steps

Update me!

1 Visit the WWW site for the vendor.

2 Locate the page for new drivers.

3 Find your driver and click on its name.

4 Save the file in a temporary folder.

5 Using the Windows Explorer, click on the file to expand it.

6 Install NT and when prompted, point to this temporary folder containing the device driver.

Whenever you update an operating system, it's quite likely that some of the drivers used by devices, such as the CD-ROM, SCSI or display will need updating.

These drivers can be found either on the NT CD-ROM or you may have to visit the vendor's WWW site to download the latest copy.

The best approach is to try to install NT first and if it doesn't work, then go hunt for the driver. But it's most likely you won't need to do any searching.

If you visit the vendor's WWW site, they should have an area called something like support or software/hardware downloads. If you don't have access to the WWW then call their support line and they should be able to help you.

New drivers are usually packed in executable files. So once it is downloaded to your machine, run it, to obtain the new files and then you are ready to install it.

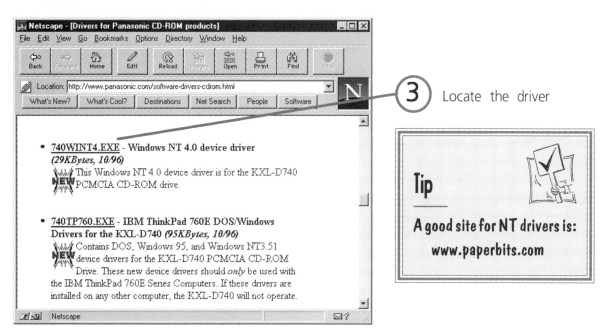

3 Locate the driver

Tip

A good site for NT drivers is: **www.paperbits.com**

Installing

Installing NT is very easy, just be prepared to answer a few questions, swap disks and be patient, because it requires longer than a few minutes to complete the task.

If you have never installed an operating system before, don't worry, you will feel like an expert after this!

Windows NT is installed from a cold machine. That is, put the first floppy disk in the drive and switch on the computer. This will force the computer to read the floppy disk first and begin the setup process for NT. After a short while you will see *Welcome to Setup* and be asked many questions at different times. While all the files are being copied, you can stretch your legs, but don't stay away too long because there will be more questions for you to answer.

Do create an Emergency Repair Disk. This contains a copy of your system configuration. It can be used to regain access to your system in the event of a major failure.

Finally, you will be asked to remove all floppy disks and click on the restart icon with the mouse. The computer will restart and Windows NT will start. You will be greeted with the Windows NT screen and asked to hit [Cntrl] + [Alt] + [Delete] to logon. Now the fun will start, welcome to Windows NT.

1 Insert Setup Disk 1 into the floppy disk drive and switch on the computer.

2 Insert the floppy disks and CD-ROM as requested.

3 Answer all the questions about the computer.

4 Create the Emergency Repair Disk

5 Restart the computer to complete the installation.

Tip

Don't ever lose the CD Key or you won't be able to install the software

Basic steps

1 Answer all the questions on the screen.

2 Click on **Next>** for the next page.

3 Click on **Finish** when done.

A **Wizard** is a step-by-step guide to completing a task. When a task has to be performed in NT, sometimes a wizard is provided to enable you to complete the task easily. Wizards are not always available, but when one is offered to you, use it, because it takes you through the steps one-by-one by requesting that you answer the questions displayed on the screen.

Some of the tasks that have wizards include:

- add a new printer
- create a shortcut
- add/remove programs
- add a modem

NT doesn't always tell you that you are using a wizard, but any task that involves you answering questions on a number of screens can be considered a wizard. For a detailed example, see *Add a printer* in Chapter 5.

The add printer wizard

① Answer the questions

The wizard for installing a new modem.

Click on Next

② Click on Next

Summary

❑ **MSDOS** was one of the first operating systems for personal computers.

❑ **GUI** based operating systems, such as Windows, make communicating with the computer so much easier.

❑ Windows NT can run **multiple tasks** at the same time.

❑ NT can be run on **computers other** than those using the Intel computer chip, unlike Windows 95 which can only be run on Intel or similar chips.

❑ **Windows 95** has the same graphical interface as Windows NT 4.0.

❑ **Windows NT** may look the same as Windows 95 but it offers much more functionality.

❑ **Windows NT Workstation** should be more than adequate for home users and some business users.

❑ **Verify** your computer is suitable to run Windows NT.

❑ Use the **NTFS** file system, unless you want to share your files with Windows 3.1 or 95 users.

❑ Read the **installation guide** before you install.

❑ **Installation** is simple, but it will probably take at least 15 minutes.

2 Getting started

Which one?

One of the advantages of using Windows NT is that it can be installed on a disk that contains other operating systems such as Windows 95.

When you start the computer, it will go through its normal startup procedure, then it will present you with a list of the available operating systems. By default, it will wait for 30 seconds, giving you time to choose which one you want.

Simply select the operating system you require and the computer will do the rest.

Basic steps

1 Switch on the computer.

2 Watch it go through the normal starting sequence.

3 Select from the list of available operating systems and press [Enter].

③ Select the Operating system

```
OS Loader V4.00
Please select the operating system to start:

Windows NT Workstation Version 4.00
Windows NT Workstation Version 4.00    [VGA mode]
Microsoft Windows


Use ↑ and ↓ to move the highlight to your choice.
Press Enter to choose.
```

Tip

You can only run more than one operating system if the disk has been formatted in such a way that each operating system can use it.

Take note

NT always creates two versions to install. Don't use the one marked [VGA mode] unless you cannot start NT using one of the other listed options.

Basic steps

1 Switch on the computer and wait for the **Begin logon** dialog box to appear.

2 Press the keys [Crtl] – [Alt] – [Delete].

3 Type in your username and password.

To use Windows NT you must first log on to the computer. This may be a new concept for some users and simply involves entering your username and password.

A username is a unique name that you present to the computer to identify yourself. It can consist of up to 20 upper or lower case characters.

The password can comprise up to 14 characters, and must not have been defined by any other user on the system. Passwords are case-sensitive, therefore 'Telescope' is not the same as 'TELESCOPE' or 'telescope'.

The username and password are first created by the person responsible for creating new users. Once created anyone can usually change their own password.

Take note

Your username determines the applic-ations you may use. So don't be surprised if another user can run the applications on your Start menu.

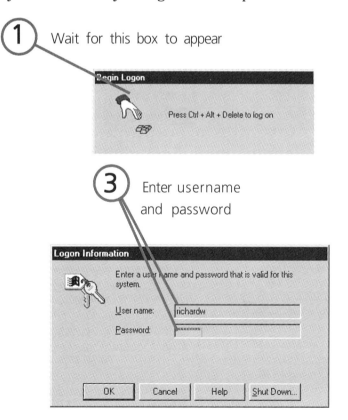

(1) Wait for this box to appear

Begin Logon

Press Ctrl + Alt + Delete to log on

(3) Enter username and password

Logon Information

Enter a user name and password that is valid for this system.

User name: richardw

Password: ××××××××

OK   Cancel   Help   Shut Down...

Help me!

Windows NT is supplied with very few manuals for you to read. Therefore anyone using it will frequently refer to Help, which is never very far away. You can find help in a number of places:

● Select Help from the Start menu.

● All applications provide access to Help.

● Context help from dialog boxes.

● Press the [F1] key.

Basic steps

❑ From the Desktop

1 Click 🏁 **Start**

2 Click on **Help**

❑ From an Application

1 Click on **Help** on the menu bar

2 Select **Help** topics

Desktop

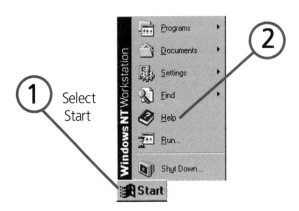

Select Start

Select Help

Tip

Since Windows NT comes with virtually no manuals, read this book first to become acquainted with the many features in NT.

Application

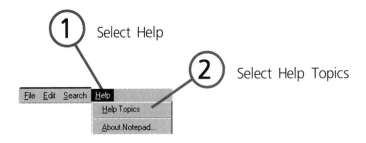

Select Help

Select Help Topics

Basic steps

Context

❏ Context Help

1 Click on the ?

2 Drag the ? icon over to the subject and click.

3 Help box appears.

4 Click anywhere to remove the Help box.

Return to Step 2 to obtain help on any other item in the window.

Context help is one of the fastest ways to get information. It's available whenever you see the ? icon on the Title Bar. The best way to use it, is to click over the item you want information on, alternatively you can press the function key [F1].

Context help is usually found on dialog boxes. Take the example below, the user is asked to supply the computer name, but doesn't understand what it means. Context help displays the meaning of what is required.

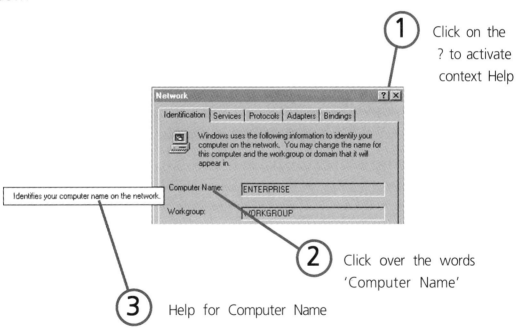

① Click on the ? to activate context Help

② Click over the words 'Computer Name'

③ Help for Computer Name

Application help

Application help is the one that you will use most of the time. Think of using Help like you would a book. First check the Contents page to see the headings of each chapter. Navigate down the hierarchy of pages to find the one that you are interested in.

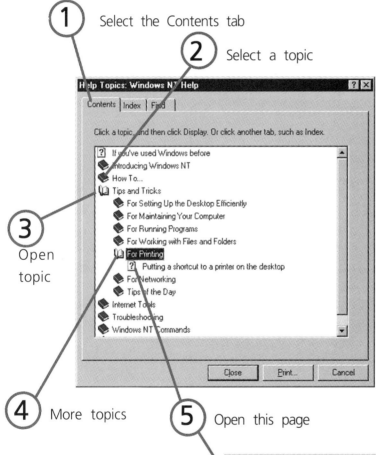

① Select the Contents tab

② Select a topic

③ Open topic

④ More topics

⑤ Open this page

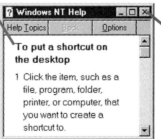

⑥ Close the window

1 Click on the **Contents** tab.

2 Review the contents list and double click on the 📖 icon to see the topics within the chapter.

3 The book is now open – denoted by the 📖 icon.

4 Review the contents list and double click on the 📖 to see more topics on this subject

or

5 Review the contents list and double click on the ? icon to read the help.

6 Click on the ✕ to close the window.

Basic steps

1 Click on the **Index** tab.

2 Type the first letters from the word into the first box.

3 Review the list of topics and double click on the one of interest or click on the Display button

4 Click on the ☒ to close the window.

Sometimes you may find it quicker to use the Index. If you think about what you do when you read a paper book, how often do you go straight to the index to see if the topic you are interested in is referenced? Well, the index in help works exactly the same.

Tip

Don't forget to use the scroll bar to move through the list quickly.

① Select the Index tab

② Type some letters or words

③ Double click on a topic

④ Close the window

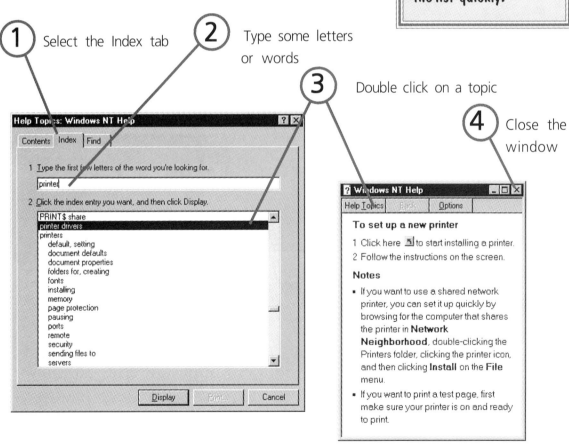

Help me find it

If you are lucky, then you may find what you are looking for by searching the Contents or the Index. If today is not your lucky day, then instead trying searching through all the documents using the Find facility.

1 Click on the **Find** tab.

2 Enter letters or words into the top slot.

3 Select a topic in the middle pane to reduce the list of topics in the bottom pane.

4 Double click on the topic which matches the subject you are looking for.

5 If there are no useful topics in the bottom pane, return to Step 2 and try again.

① Select the Find tab

② Enter letters or words

③ Select to reduce the list of topics

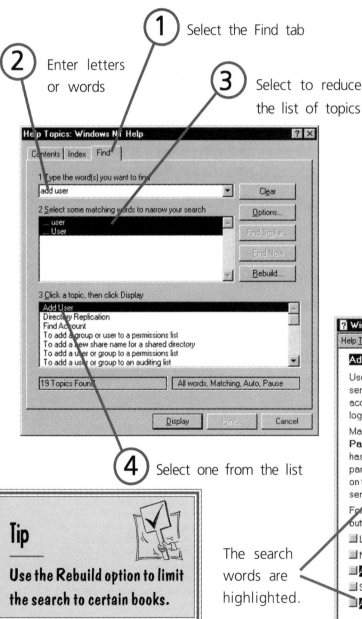

④ Select one from the list

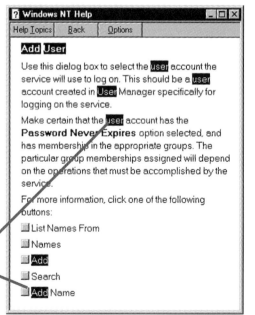

The search words are highlighted.

Tip

Use the Rebuild option to limit the search to certain books.

❑ **Log Off**

1 Click on the ▨**Start** button.

2 Click on **Shutdown**.

3 Select **Close all programs and log on as a different user** .

❑ **Shutdown**

1 Click on the ▨**Start** button.

2 Click on Shutdown.

3 Select **shutdown the computer** .

❑ **Lock the workstation**

1 Press **[Ctrl]** – **[Alt]** – **[Delete]** together.

2 Click on the **Lock Workstation** button.

When you have finished working, several options are available to the user:

● Close the user session by logging off.

● Shutdown the computer.

● Lock the Workstation.

So which one do you choose? Well, if you won't be using the computer again then select shutdown and switch it off. If you will return to the computer later then two options are available.

Locking the Workstation permits the user to leave the computer as it is, ready for immediate use with the applications running, but locked, so that no other person can use it. This is a good choice because it leaves your desktop exactly as it is currently.

Logging off closes all of your programs and resets the computer so that it is ready for another user to log in.

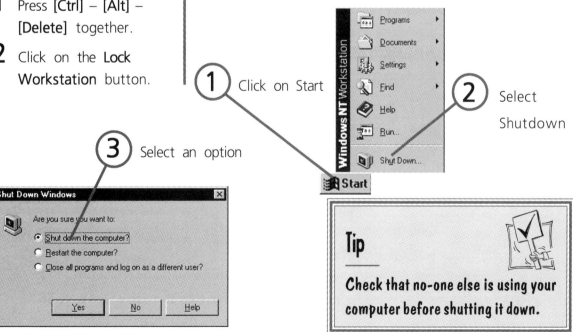

① Click on Start

② Select Shutdown

③ Select an option

Tip

Check that no-one else is using your computer before shutting it down.

NT Explorer

If you have used Windows for Workgroup or previous versions of Windows NT, you are probably familiar with the File Manager. In this version of NT, the File Manager has been replaced by Windows NT Explorer. Throughout this book you will often see displays from NT Explorer, therefore now is the time to become familiar with what it can do. NT Explorer can do much more than just copy files around because you can also:

- specify which applications a user can run (page 58)
- see all the computers and printers on the network (page 104)
- invoke the Control Panel (page 37)
- see all the printers that are available (page 69)
- connect to a network drive (page 106)
- empty the Recycle Bin (page 86)
- view the contents of the Briefcase (page 120)
- create folders (page 31)

Basic steps

1 Click on 🪟 Start and select **Programs** then **Windows NT Explorer**.

or

1 Click on the [Explorer] icon on the desktop.

2 Click on **My Computer** to see all the disks attached to the computer.

3 Select **View**

4 Select **Large icons**

5 Select **Small icons**

6 Select **List**

7 Select **Detail**

Expand to see the files and folders on your computer

Expand to see the computers on the network

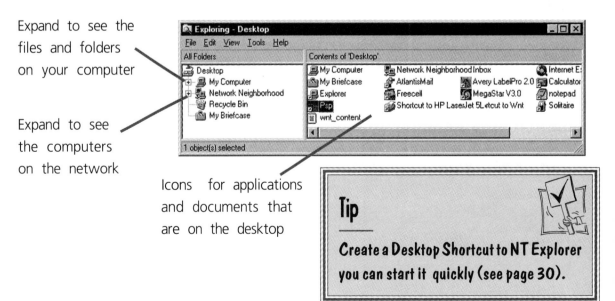

Icons for applications and documents that are on the desktop

Tip

Create a Desktop Shortcut to NT Explorer you can start it quickly (see page 30).

26

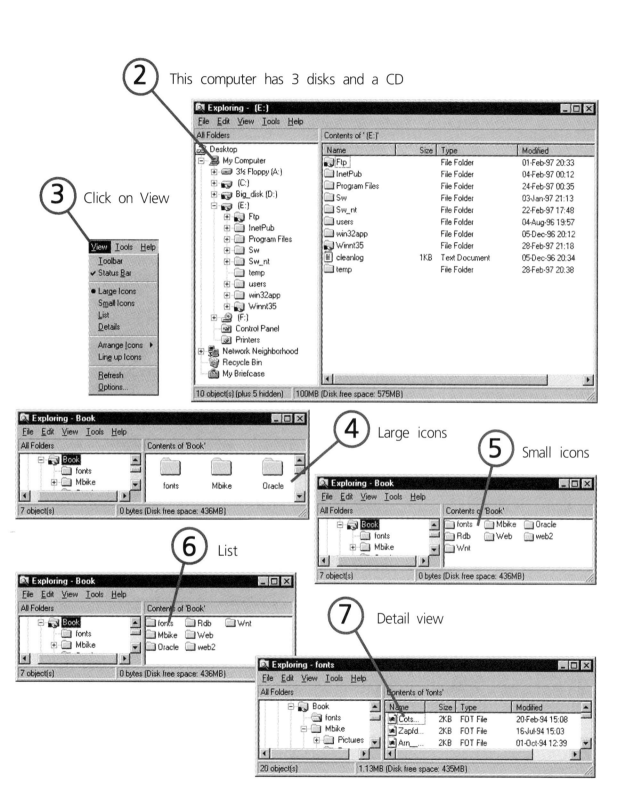

② This computer has 3 disks and a CD

③ Click on View

④ Large icons

⑤ Small icons

⑥ List

⑦ Detail view

27

The Desktop

What does your desk look like? Now be honest, it is probably slightly untidy with papers that you are reading on it and things that you are using like pens, paper and diary close to hand. Sound familiar? Then how would you like to organise the things you do on the computer the same way, but without the chaos.

Instead of running a program from the Start menu, an icon representing the application can be placed on the Desktop. Any document that you are reading can also be placed on the Desktop. The icons on the Desktop can be placed wherever you like, so it's time to have fun and organise your Desktop. It's entirely up to you how it is laid out.

The fastest way to place a document or application is to the use the drag and drop technique. Alternatively you can create a Shortcut which is described in the next section.

Basic steps

1 Find the object to put on the desktop.

2 Press the right mouse button while over the object and drag it to the desktop.

3 When the object is on the desktop at the position where you want it to be, release the mouse button.

4 Select **Create Shortcut** from the menu.

5 Edit the name.

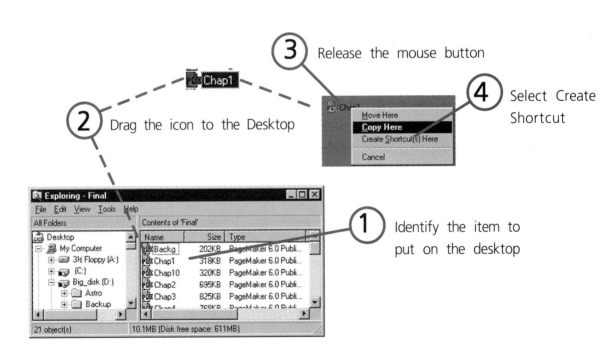

(3) Release the mouse button

(4) Select Create Shortcut

(2) Drag the icon to the Desktop

(1) Identify the item to put on the desktop

28

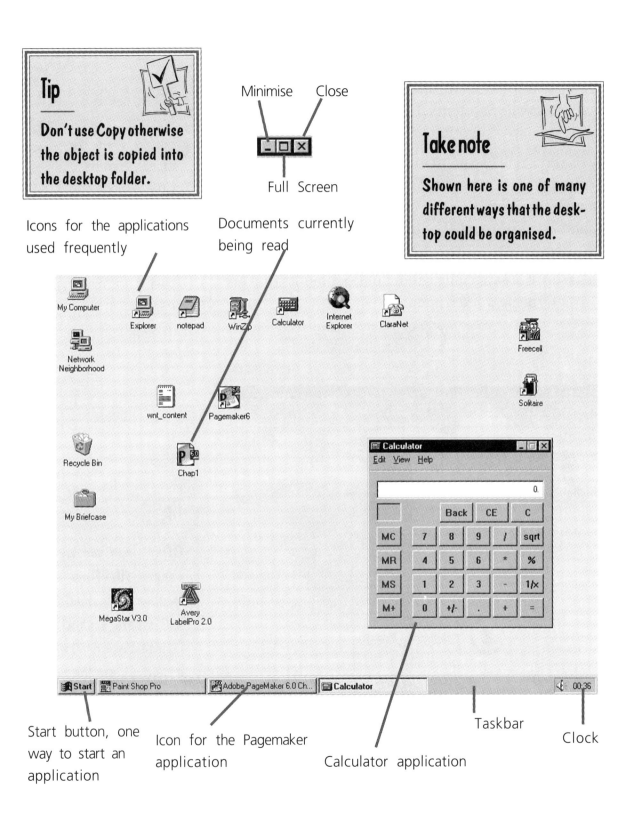

Tip

Don't use Copy otherwise the object is copied into the desktop folder.

Minimise   Close

Full Screen

Take note

Shown here is one of many different ways that the desktop could be organised.

Icons for the applications used frequently

Documents currently being read

My Computer

Explorer   notepad   WinZip   Calculator   Internet Explorer   ClaraNet

Freecell

Network Neighborhood

wnt_content   Pagemaker6

Solitaire

Recycle Bin

Chap1

My Briefcase

MegaStar V3.0   Avery LabelPro 2.0

Calculator

Edit View Help

0.

		Back	CE	C
MC	7	8	9	/	sqrt
MR	4	5	6	*	%
MS	1	2	3	-	1/x
M+	0	+/-	.	+	=

Start | Paint Shop Pro | Adobe PageMaker 6.0 Ch... | Calculator | 00:36

Start button, one way to start an application

Icon for the Pagemaker application

Calculator application

Taskbar

Clock

Create a Shortcut

A nice feature in Windows NT and Windows 95 is the ability to create Shortcuts. They can be created any time, anywhere, so why bother?

Well a Shortcut can point to an application, a document and a folder. The big benefit is that it allows you to access documents and applications from the Desktop, rather than working through the Start menu.

One of the best places to create a Shortcut is on the Desktop. It is especially useful for documents that are currently being worked upon.

Basic steps

1 Find the object.

2 Press the right mouse button while over the object and select **Create Shortcut**.

3 Click on the shortcut icon, edit to remove the '*Shortcut to...*' and give it a meaningful name.

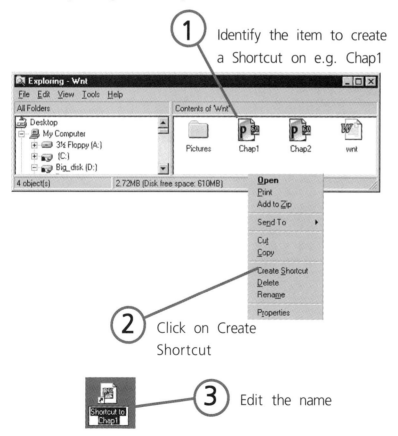

① Identify the item to create a Shortcut on e.g. Chap1

② Click on Create Shortcut

③ Edit the name

Tip

Often when you try to copy a file from one location to another, NT will create a shortcut instead. If you don't want a shortcut, use the right mouse button and request to move the file.

Basic steps

1 Start Windows NT

Explorer

2 Select location for folder.

3 Click on **File** then **New** then **Folder**

4 The Folder is created and you are prompted to change the name from *New Folder*.

Information in a computer needs to be grouped together, just like you do at home or work. How do you keep all of your credit card statements? Probably clipped together in a file. Imagine that folder inside the computer and you begin to understand how folders in Windows NT operate.

A folder is created to hold applications, files, documents or whatever you want. You can have as many folders as you like and you can create folders, within folders. (A folder is very similar to a directory in DOS.)

How many folder should you create? That is entirely up to you and how you like to organise things.

(1) Start Explorer

(2) Select the location

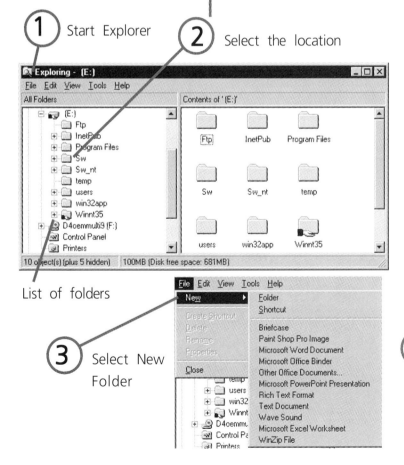

List of folders

(3) Select New Folder

Tip

A Shortcut for a folder can be placed on the Desktop. Then you can go to your favourite folders without having to open NT Explorer first.

(4) Edit the Folder Name

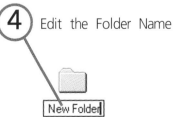

New Folder

The Taskbar

Once you start using Windows NT, take a moment to become acquainted with the Taskbar. This contains the Start button and all the applications that are running on the computer, represented as buttons. Simply click on the button to restart that application.

The clock is usually present in its own box. Depending on what you are doing, icons will appear in that box, such as a speaker and a modem. For instance, clicking on the speaker icon will bring up the speaker properties. The modem is another useful icon, because you can see the lights flash when data is transmitted and received.

The Taskbar can be customised in several ways. For example, it can be hidden off an edge of the screen, reappearing when the mouse is moved to that edge.

Basic steps

1 Right click on any blank space on the Taskbar.

2 Select **Properties**.

3 Click **Auto Hide** to hide the Taskbar, and click OK.

4 Move the mouse goes over the location where the Taskbar would reside to make it reappear..

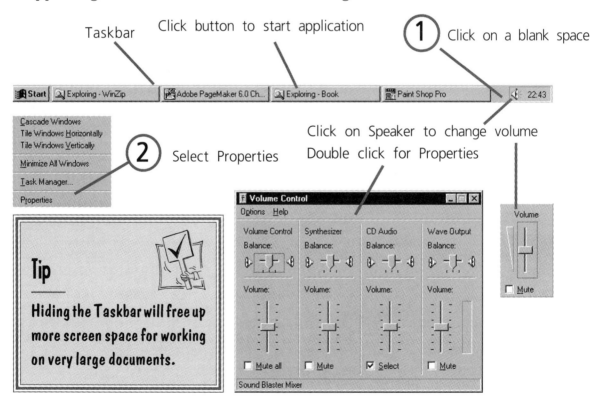

Taskbar Click button to start application ① Click on a blank space

② Select Properties

Click on Speaker to change volume
Double click for Properties

Tip

Hiding the Taskbar will free up more screen space for working on very large documents.

32

Basic steps

5 Change options such as **Show Clock** to prevent the clock being displayed.

6 Click on **OK** when finished.

Tip

The taskbar doesn't have to be located at the bottom of the screen. It can be moved to any of the sides of the desktop by dragging it to its new location.

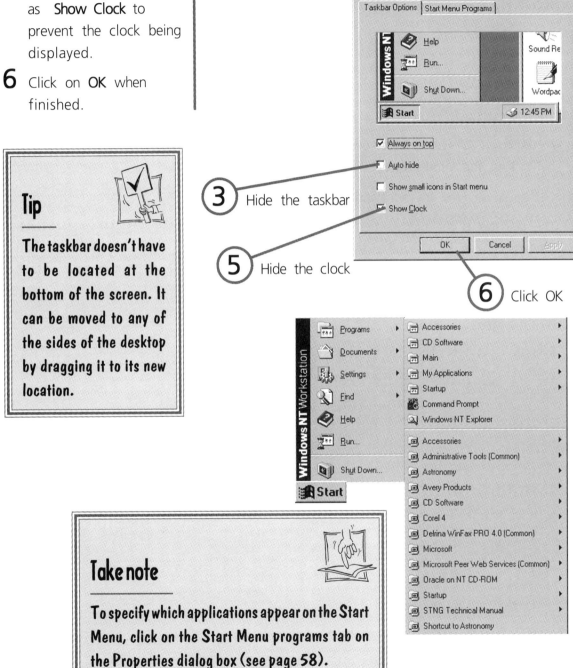

③ Hide the taskbar

⑤ Hide the clock

⑥ Click OK

Take note

To specify which applications appear on the Start Menu, click on the Start Menu programs tab on the Properties dialog box (see page 58).

Summary

- ❑ The computer can run **multiple operating systems** such as Windows NT and Windows '95.

- ❑ To use NT you first **log on** using a username and password.

- ❑ There are several different ways to get **help**.

- ❑ To finish using NT you must **log off**.

- ❑ A Windows NT session can be temporarily suspended by **locking the Workstation**.

- ❑ Get to know how to use **Windows NT Explorer**.

- ❑ The **desktop** is the place where applications and documents can be started quickly.

- ❑ A **Shortcut** is a means to quickly access applications and documents from a location other than their home.

- ❑ Everything in the computer is held in **folders**.

- ❑ The **Taskbar** contains all the running applications.

3 Configuring NT

My Computer

When Windows NT is installed, an icon is created in the top left-hand corner called **My Computer** which when clicked provides you with a staring point for the following information about your computer.

- disk drives
- floppy disks
- printers
- all the settings for dial-up networking
- icon to the Control Panel, where the system configuration is held and from where it can be amended

An alternative place to find this information is Windows NT Explorer, but the icon on the desktop is possibly a quicker route and easier to read. Look at NT Explorer and decide for yourself which method you prefer.

Basic steps

1 Click on the icon **My Computer**.

2 Click on the icon for the item you are interested in.

or

1 Click on **Start** and from **Programs** select **Windows NT Explorer**

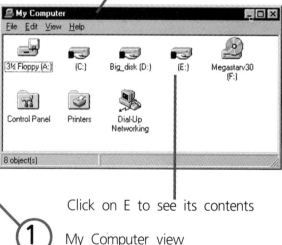

② My Computer folder

① My Computer icon on the desktop

Click on E to see its contents

① My Computer view from NT Explorer

Contents same view in Step 2

Basic steps

1 Click on

2 Click on **Control Panel**

or

1 Click on **Start** and from **Programs** select **NT Explorer**. Scroll and click on the icon for **Control Panel**.

The Control Panel

If you have worked with any version of Windows before, then the Control Panel will be familiar to you. It is very important and you should become familiar with its contents and what it can do for you. Just say to yourself, do I want to configure something on the computer. If the answer is yes, then head straight for the control panel.

In this chapter we will look at how to configure a number of important components in the computer. All you have to do is click on the icon which represents the item of interest and the configuration application will start.

Configuring most items is fairly straightfoward. Answer the questions and NT will do the rest. Sometimes NT will request that the computer be restarted, so that the changes can take effect. If at any time you make a mistake, usually you can undo the changes by hitting the Cancel button.

Control Panel

Some of the most useful icons are:

● Display

● Modems

● Mouse

● Network

● Printers

● Services

● System

Devices

Hopefully the Devices panel will be one that you won't have to use very often. Nevertheless, it's a good idea to be familiar with how it operates and when it might be necessary to use it.

The Devices panel lists all the devices such as CD-ROM, floppy, SCSI controller, mouse, keyboard and whether they have been started.

This is a useful panel to use if you have any system problems. For example, suppose the modem isn't working. First check this panel and see if the device has been started. If it has not, this could be the cause of your problem. So start the modem here bt selecting the device and clicking **Start**, then try again.

1 From the Control Panel click on Devices

2 Scroll through the list and find the device. Then check its status.

3 Start or stop the device as required.

4 Click on close when done.

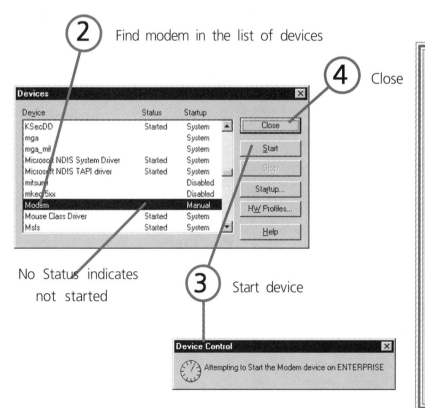

② Find modem in the list of devices

④ Close

No Status indicates not started

③ Start device

Tip

Don't enable or disable a device unless you are completely certain that you have selected the right one, and that the change will not prevent the computer from starting. If the computer won't start, then choose one of the hardware profiles that does work.

Basic steps

1 From **Help** search for **Emergency Repair Disk**.

or

1 Click on **Start** then click on **Run** and enter **rdisk**.

2 Select whether to update or create a new repair disk.

3 Insert the floppy disk into the drive.

4 When finished remove the floppy disk and label it, *Emergency Repair Disk* and the date.

When NT was first installed, an Emergency Repair Disk should have been created. This contains a copy of your configuration and can be used by NT to help recover your system in the event of an emergency.

This information is held on a floppy disk and therefore forms a vital part of system backup. Whenever your system configuration changes, such as:

● add a new disk

● change disk letters

● added a new device

the Emergency Repair Disk should be updated.

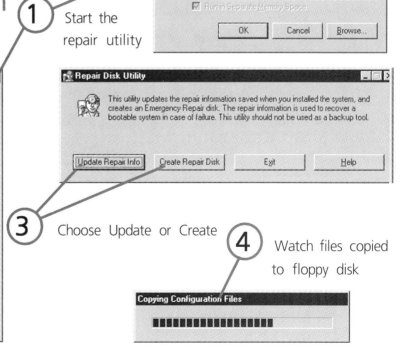

① Start the repair utility

Using the Repair Disk utility to make an emergency repair disk

The Repair Disk utility saves all of your current system settings to an Emergency Repair Disk (ERD). You can then use this disk to restore your computer if files become damaged.

It is strongly recommended that you create and update an ERD every time you make significant changes to your hardware or software setup.

To start Repair Disk

▶ Click here

For information about how to use Repair Disk, click the **Help** menu in Repair Disk.

③ Choose Update or Create

④ Watch files copied to floppy disk

Display

This is one of the system configuration components that may be changed frequently. From here, the user specifies:

- screen background
- screen saver
- how the windows look
- desktop options
- monitor settings

To modify any of these items, click on the required tab and make the necessary changes, it's that simple. Don't be afraid to change the background or screen saver frequently, because that is part of the fun of using a computer.

Of course, if your company provides an official background or screen svaer, then changes won't be possible.

Basic steps

1 Click on 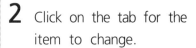 icon.

2 Click on the tab for the item to change.

3 Select your options at the dialog box.

4 Click **OK** when done.

(2) Change the screen saver

(3) Use this one

(2) Change the background

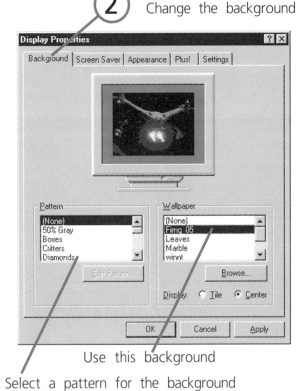

Use this background

Select a pattern for the background

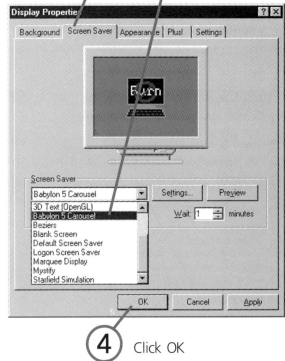

(4) Click OK

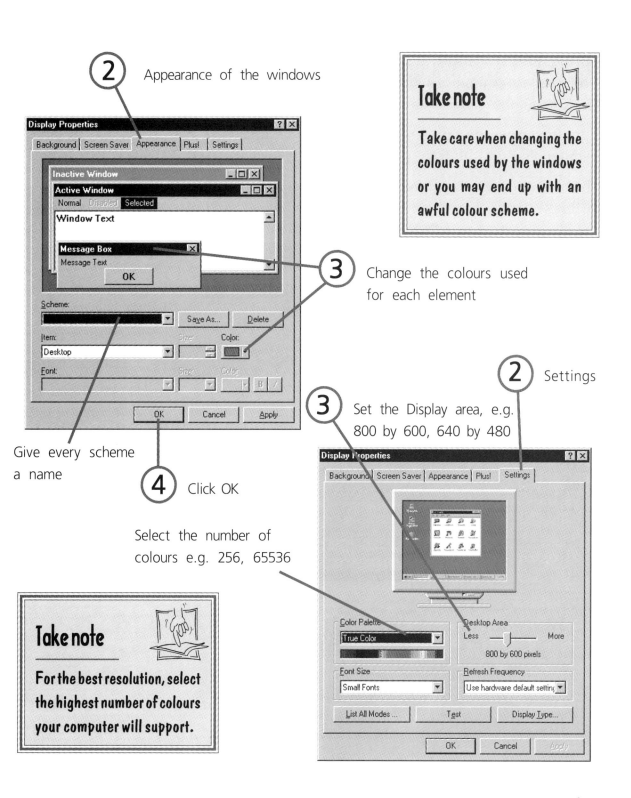

(2) Appearance of the windows

Take note

Take care when changing the colours used by the windows or you may end up with an awful colour scheme.

(3) Change the colours used for each element

Give every scheme a name

(4) Click OK

(2) Settings

(3) Set the Display area, e.g. 800 by 600, 640 by 480

Select the number of colours e.g. 256, 65536

Take note

For the best resolution, select the highest number of colours your computer will support.

41

Regional settings

During the installation NT will choose a country onto which to base computer settings like the format of dates and how numbers are displayed.

If you have a personal preference, such as no commas in number displays, this is the place to define the format.

The settings here will apply to all the applications running on this system.

Basic steps

1 Click on the icon Regional Settings

2 Click on the tab to select the setting to change.

3 Modify the settings as required.

4 Click on **OK** or the **Apply** button for the changes to take effect.

(2) Select the setting

Regional Settings Properties

Regional Settings | Number | Currency | Time | Date | Input Locales

Many programs support international settings. Changing the Regional Settings affects the way these programs display and sort dates, times, currency, and numbers.

English (United Kingdom)

(3) Pick a country

(3) Pick or define a date format

(3) Define format

Regional Settings | Number | Currency | Time | Date | Input Locales

Calendar type: Gregorian Calendar

Short date

Short date sample: 26-Jan-97

Short date style: dd-MMM-yy
- dd-MMM-yy
- dd/MM/yy
- d/M/yy
- d.M.yy

Date separator: -

Long date

Long date sample: 26 January 1997

Long date style: dd MMMM yyyy

Regional Settings | Number | Currency | Time | Date | Input Locales

Appearance samples

Positive: £123,456,789.00   Negative: -£123,456,789.00

¤ = Universal currency symbol

Currency symbol: £

Positive currency format: ¤1.1

Negative currency format: -¤1.1

Decimal symbol: .

No. of digits after decimal: 2

Digit grouping symbol:

No. of digits in group: 3

OK | Cancel | Apply

(4) OK when done

42

1 Click on the icon

2 Select the action.

3 Find the sound.

4 Repeat steps 2 and 3 for every action.

5 Give a name to this sound configuration.

6 Click on **OK** to finish.

NT lets you have a bit of fun with your computer when it comes to sounds. For example, when a user logged in, the system could say, 'Welcome - have a nice day' or some other appropriate greeting.

Sounds can be assigned to many actions, and can be any WAV file. There are some supplied with NT, you cam also use those that you have obtained – or created – yourself. (See *Multimedia Made Simple* for creating WAV files.)

It may be that on one day a particular sound is suitable, and tomorrow another is required. Therefore take the opportunity to name each of these schemes so they can easily be reused over and over again.

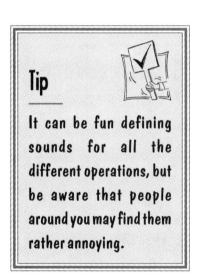

Tip

It can be fun defining sounds for all the different operations, but be aware that people around you may find them rather annoying.

Take note

Many ftp sites offer sound files for downloading. If you can't find the ones you require, ask in one of the alt.binaries.sound newsgroups.

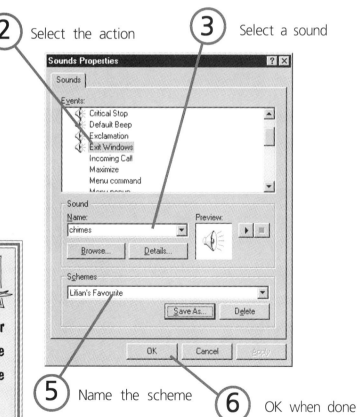

(2) Select the action

(3) Select a sound

(5) Name the scheme

(6) OK when done

Services

We have already seen that a device such as a modem may not be available because it has not been started. Services are another component that must be considered when troubleshooting an application.

A service is a software routine that performs a specific function. NT creates a number of them and when you install software such as a database system, then it will create services that it requires.

Usually these services are self-managing – that is, they are configured to start and stop automatically. Hence the users of the system need never know that they are there.

However, sometimes certain services may need to be stopped while software is being installed. Therefore it is wise to know how to deal with them.

Basic steps

1 Click the ✿ icon.
Services

2 Find the service in the list and check its status.

3 **Start**, **Stop** or **Pause** the service as required.

4 Confirm the action and watch the status change.

5 Optionally click on **Startup** to define when service starts.

6 Set the **Startup Type**.

7 Click **OK** when done.

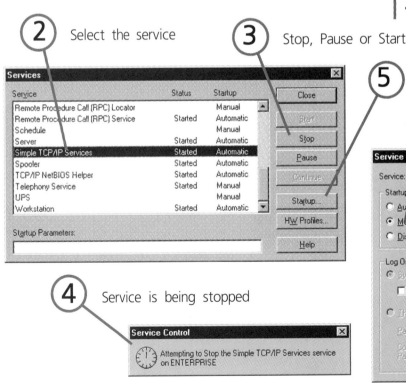

② Select the service

③ Stop, Pause or Start

⑤ Redefine Startup

⑥ Select Startup Type

④ Service is being stopped

44

Basic steps

1 Click the **Services** icon.

2 Click on **HW Profiles**.

or

1 Click the **System** icon.

2 Click on the tab **Hardware Profiles**.

3 For the configuration selected press the **Copy** button.

4 Name the configuration and click **OK**.

A very useful feature that is available in NT is the ability to define hardware profiles. There is no editing to do because the profile is defined, based on how the hardware is currently connected. All that is needed is a name for the configuration.

Why would you want different hardware profiles? Well, suppose that to do backups of the system you borrow a tape drive. When the tape drive is attached, a hardware profile is created called *Tape Drive*. When it is not attached, there is another profile called *No Tape Drive*. Whenever the system starts, you are prompted to select which hardware profile to use. Using this method, NT doesn't report annoying error messages such as *Device not found*.

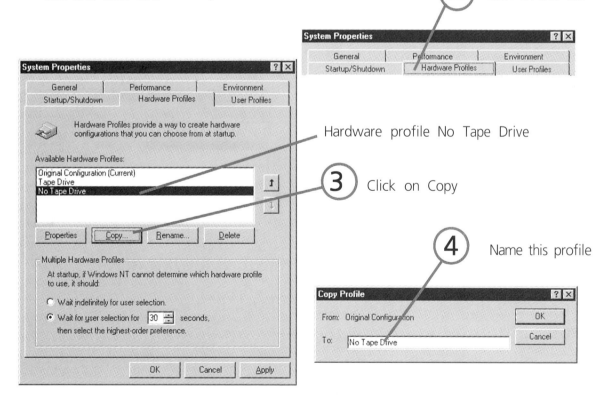

2 Click on this tab

Hardware profile No Tape Drive

3 Click on Copy

4 Name this profile

Virtual memory

Virtual memory is space on disk that is used in conjunction with the computer's main memory, to hold the information needed by the active applications. NT will swap the information from the main to the virtual memory, back and forth as it is needed. This gives the computer more memory to use and it's a good idea to create a large virtual memory file. 100Mb is probably a good starting point, but it depends upon the applications run on the computer. At any time, the file's size can be changed and it will take effect the next time the computer is started.

Basic steps

1 Click the 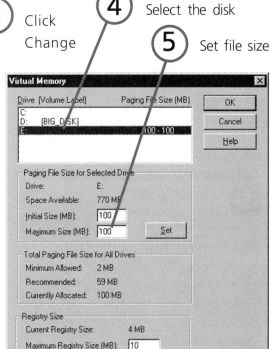 **System** icon.

2 Open the **Performance** tab.

3 In **Virtual Memory** click the **Change** button.

4 Select the disk drive for the virtual memory file.

5 Specify the size of the file and click **Set**.

6 Click **OK** when done.

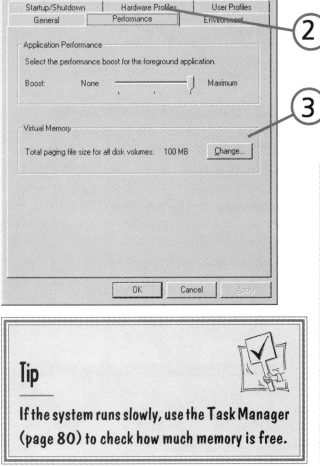

② Open Performance

③ Click Change

④ Select the disk

⑤ Set file size

Tip

If the system runs slowly, use the Task Manager (page 80) to check how much memory is free.

Basic steps

1 Click the icon Add/Remove Programs

2 Click on the tab **Install/Uninstall**.

3 Select the application from the list.

4 Click the **Add/Remove** button.

5 Confirm the program is to be removed.

Remove me!

How often have you installed some software and then decided that you don't want it any more? Some software today comes with an Uninstall icon. If you can't see one, then Windows NT may be able to help you.

This is a very safe method for removing software because it invokes the vendor's procedure for removing it. If the software doesn't have a delete routine, then applications must be carefully deleted manually.

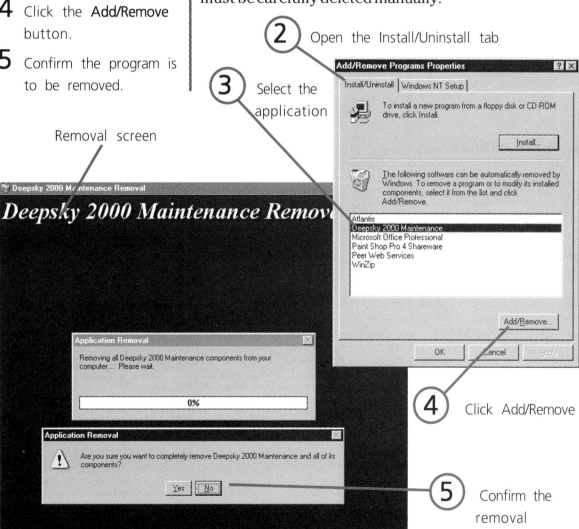

Removal screen

(2) Open the Install/Uninstall tab

(3) Select the application

(4) Click Add/Remove

(5) Confirm the removal

Summary

- Use **My Computer** to see the disks, CD-ROM drives and other aspects of your computer.

- The **Control Panel** contains all the icons to configure the components of the system.

- If a component isn't working, check the **devices** screen to see that it is running.

- Always update the **Emergency Repair Disk** whenever you make major change to the system configuration.

- Choose a **background** from the display icon.

- The **formats of dates and numbers**, used by all applications can be changed from the regional settings icon.

- **Sound configurations** can be named so they can be easily retrieved.

- If applications fail to run, check that the **Services** associated with that application are running.

- Create **hardware profiles** if you configure your system with different devices.

- Create a large **virtual memory** file.

- Remove applications using the **Add/Remove** programs option.

4 Users

What is a user?

We have already seen that before you can use a computer running Windows NT, you must first logon with a username and password. The reason for this is that a computer running Windows NT is designed to be used by many people. The username prevents people having access to other users' files and running applications that they are not allowed to.

The username is created by the person who administers the computer. They will also advise the password required to log on, however, you can usually change the password at any time, but not the username.

Tip

If you want to know the username used to log on, at any time, press the Ctrl and Alt and Delete keys together.

Applications only available to user HOBBS

Applications only available to user LILIAN

Applications available to all users

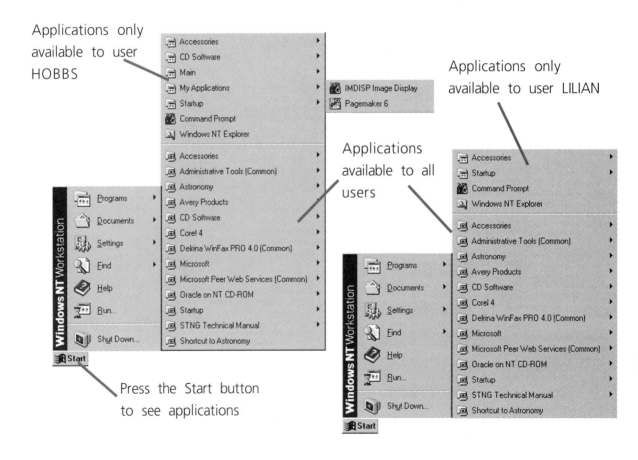

Press the Start button to see applications

Password rules

1 Click on **Start** from **Programs** click on **Administrative Tools (Common)** and then click on **User Manager**.

2 Click on **Policies**, then **Account**.

3 Change the various options.

Before creating the usernames for the people who will be using your computer, first decide what restrictions you want to place on the passwords that your users specify. Windows NT provides a number of options, which you can change at any time. But good ones to define initially are:

● How often passwords should be changed. To stop security breaches, passwords should be changed frequently.

● A minimum password length, of say 6 characters, makes it difficult for people to guess your password.

● An account can be locked if a user fails to guess their password after a specific number of attempts.

● Passwords can be remembered by NT, by setting the Password Uniqueness option, which forces the user to create a new one!

Force passwords to change

Set a minimum password length

Stop account use on bad password

Enable keeping passwords

Account Policy

Computer: ENTERPRISE

OK
Cancel
Help

Password Restrictions

Maximum Password Age
- ○ Password Never Expires
- ● Expires In [30] Days

Minimum Password Age
- ● Allow Changes Immediately
- ○ Allow Changes In [ ] Days

Minimum Password Length
- ○ Permit Blank Password
- ● At Least [6] Characters

Password Uniqueness
- ○ Do Not Keep Password History
- ● Remember [15] Passwords

- ○ No account lockout
- ● Account lockout

Lockout after [5] bad logon attempts
Reset count after [30] minutes

Lockout Duration
- ○ Forever (until admin unlocks)
- ● Duration [30] minutes

☐ Users must log on in order to change password

Add a new username

When Windows NT is first installed, three usernames are created. The most powerful is Administrator, but you won't want to give this username to general users.

Therefore it will be necessary to create some new usernames. You can create as many as you like, the only restriction is that every username must be unique.

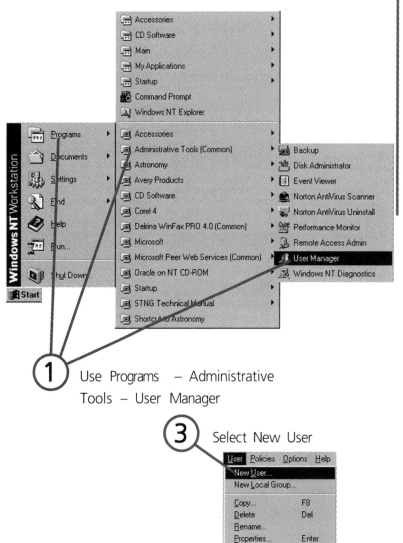

Use Programs – Administrative Tools – User Manager

Select New User

Basic steps

1 From the 🏁Start menu select **Programs** then **Administrative Tools** and **User Manager**.

2 View the list of users to see that the new name does not already exist.

3 Click on **User**, then **New User**.

4 Specify the user and password.

5 Specify which **Groups** the user participates in.

6 Click on **OK** to create the user.

Take note

Your username will determine which applications and files you can use on the computer.

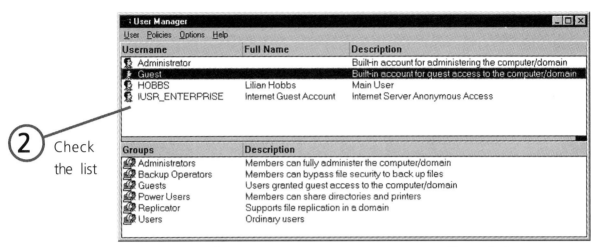

(2) Check the list

Creating a username is very easy. First define a unique name, then in the Full Name box enter the user's actual name or a suitable description if the username will be used by many users.

All usernames must have a password and most users prefer to specify it themselves. To prevent any security breach, click the box which says that the user must change the password the next time they logon.

Tip

Don't forget to specify which applications the user can run after the username has been created, as described on page 58.

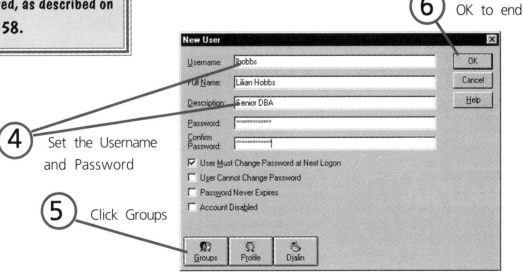

(6) OK to end

(4) Set the Username and Password

(5) Click Groups

Change me!

Sometimes you will have to change your password. It may be because NT asks you to, or you may decide that it is time to change it.

How the system has been set up, determines how frequently the password has to be changed and the minimum number of characters in the password.

When NT asks you to change the password simply enter the new one twice and the job is done. You can change the password at any time by pressing [Ctrl]–[Alt]–[Delete].

It is a good idea not to use passwords that can be easily guessed like your name or something related to a hobby. The longer the password, generally the harder it is to guess.

Passwords cannot be read, so if you forget it, then a new one has to specified. Therefore be prepared to go cap in hand to the person managing the system and request a new password. But don't worry, we have all done it at least once, especially after returning from holiday.

Take note

Change the password on the Administrator username frequently to prevent security breaches.

54

Basic steps

1 Run **User Manager**.

2 Click on **User**, then **New User Group**.

3 Enter the **Group name**.

4 Enter a description for the group.

5 Select from the list of existing users who are members of this group and press the **Add** button.

6 Click the **OK** button.

7 Review the list of users allocated to this group.

8 Click the **OK** button.

Group me!

A very useful facility is the ability to create groups of users. It is a convenient way of grouping like users together and then granting certain access rights to those users.

For example, suppose you have a number of users who wish to access your computer from the network. Instead of granting each user the right to network access, a group could be created called Remote Users. This group is given the right to access the computer from the network, then each user is allocated to this group.

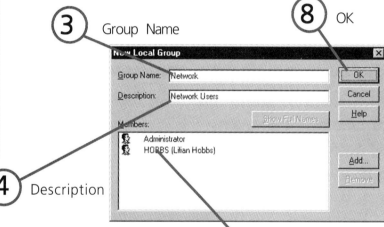

③ Group Name

⑧ OK

④ Description

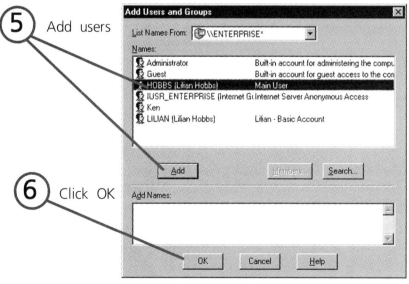

⑤ Add users

⑥ Click OK

⑦ See list of users

Your rights

Windows NT includes a list of access rights which state the actions that a group or users can perform. It is important when setting up your system and whenever you create new users, to check that they have been granted the appropriate privileges. Some of the access rights are:

- Access this computer from a network
- Backup files and directories
- Shutdown the system
- Permission to change or delete files.

Basic steps

1 Run **User Manager.**

2 Click on **Policies**, then **User Rights.**

3 Select the right to be granted.

4 Click on **Add** to see list of groups and users.

5 Select from the list of users and groups who are to receive this access right, then click the **Add** button.

6 Click the **OK** button.

7 Review the list of group and users given this access right.

8 Click the **OK** button.

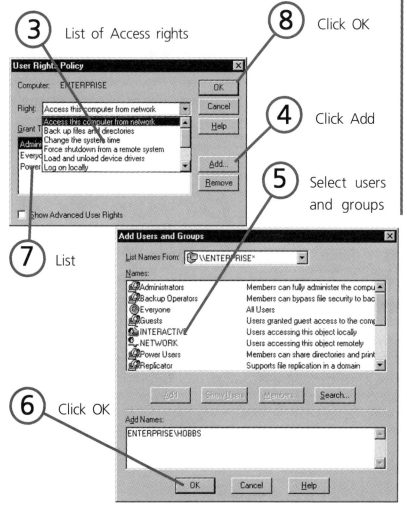

③ List of Access rights

⑧ Click OK

④ Click Add

⑤ Select users and groups

⑦ List

⑥ Click OK

Take note

The list of access rights is defined by NT.

Basic steps

Watching you

1 Run **User Manager**.

2 Click on **Policies**, then **Audit**.

3 Select the actions to be logged in the audit trail.

4 Click on **OK**.

5 From the **Start** menu select **Programs** then **Administrative Tools** then **Event Viewer**.

6 Click on **Log** then **Security** to see the security log.

Today television cameras are watching your every move. Now you can check up on what people are doing on your computer! You can audit certain events that are performed on your computer into a log. There are several different types of log (see page 76), and the contents of these can be viewed using the Event Viewer.

③ Select items to audit

④ Click OK

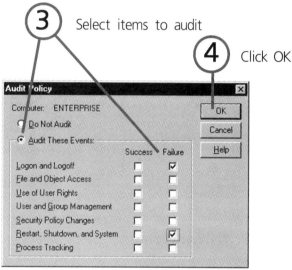

⑥ Event viewer with list of actions

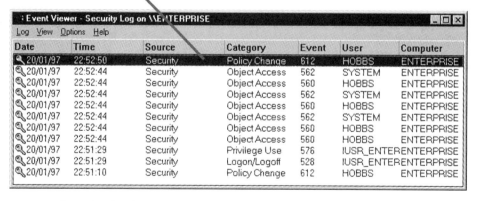

Though the log is not very specific about what was done, you can see who was doing what sort of things, and when.

What can I do?

One of the features of Windows NT is the ability to specify which applications a user can run. When an application is installed, if everyone can use it, it should be placed in the common area. If you change your mind, then it's a simple process using Explorer to say who can use the application.

All the changes that you make are instant – just click on the Start button, then Programs to see the results. But don't forget to login as that user (see page 19)!

(see page 19)

Basic steps

1 Start **NT Explorer**.

2 Locate the **Windows NT** folder.

3 Expand the folder and search for **profiles**.

4 Search the list for the username and expand to see the applications available.

5 Expand folder **Start Menu** then folder **Programs**

6 Select the application and drag and drop it into the user's folder.

7 Click on 🟦**Start**, then **Programs** to view the changes.

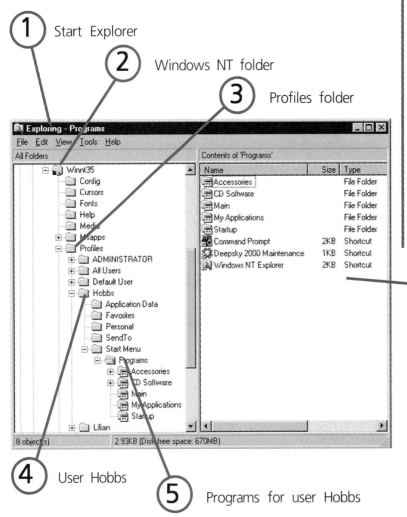

① Start Explorer

② Windows NT folder

③ Profiles folder

④ User Hobbs

⑤ Programs for user Hobbs

⑥ Drag in application

⑦ Check results

Basic steps

1 Repeat steps 1 to 3 from 'What can I do?'.

2 Expand the **All Users** folder then expand the **Start Menu** and **Programs** folders.

3 Drag the application into the list.

4 Click on ![Start], then **Programs** to view the changes.

What can we all do?

We have already seen that a user can have applications that only they can run. But most applications you will want to share so that all users can use them.

The mechanism for sharing an application is the same as for an individual user. But this time, you don't have to log out to check the Start menu, because it should be in the list of all applications.

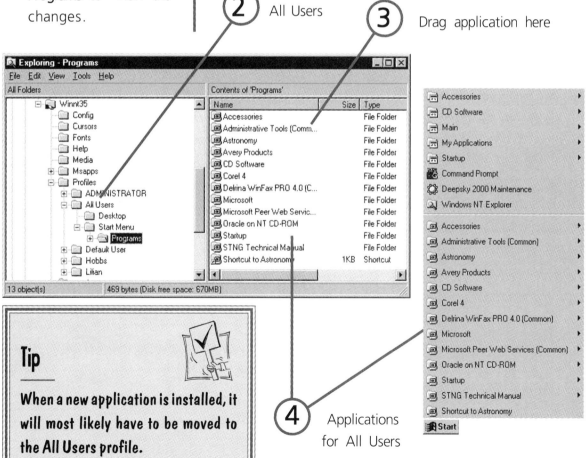

② All Users

③ Drag application here

④ Applications for All Users

Tip

When a new application is installed, it will most likely have to be moved to the All Users profile.

Summary

❑ The **username** determines the applications that a user can run.

❑ A username should have a **password**.

❑ The **account policy** should be specified to ensure passwords meet certain rules.

❑ Passwords can be **changed** at any time using the keys [Ctrl] – [Alt] – [Delete].

❑ Passwords are **case-sensitive.**

❑ **Groups** can be created, and users assigned to them.

❑ A group or user can be given certain **access rights.**

❑ Certain actions by users can be logged in an **audit trail.**

❑ An application must be moved into the **All Users** profile to be used by everyone.

5 Printers

Add a printer

Hardly anyone today has a computer without a printer. It doesn't have to be one of those fancy, high-speed laser devices. Windows NT supports hundreds of different types of printers, ranging from dot matrix, to inkjets and lasers.

A wizard will take you through the steps for setting up a printer, and you can define as many printers as you like. Provided the printer is attached to the computer, any defined printer can be printed to.

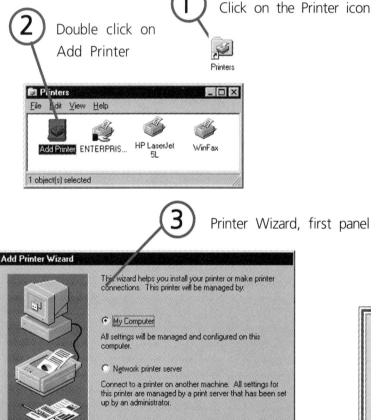

① Click on the Printer icon

② Double click on Add Printer

Printers

③ Printer Wizard, first panel

Basic steps

1 Click the Printer icon in the Control Panel.

2 Click the **Add Printer** icon.

3 The Printer Wizard starts. Select **My Computer** then click the **Next** button.

4 Select the Printer port which is usually **LPT1**.

5 Select the make then the model of printer from the list.

6 Give the printer a name.

7 Click **Yes** if you want to share your printer with other computers.

8 Print a test page.

9 Click on **Finish** to install the printer.

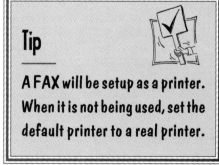

Tip

A FAX will be setup as a printer. When it is not being used, set the default printer to a real printer.

62

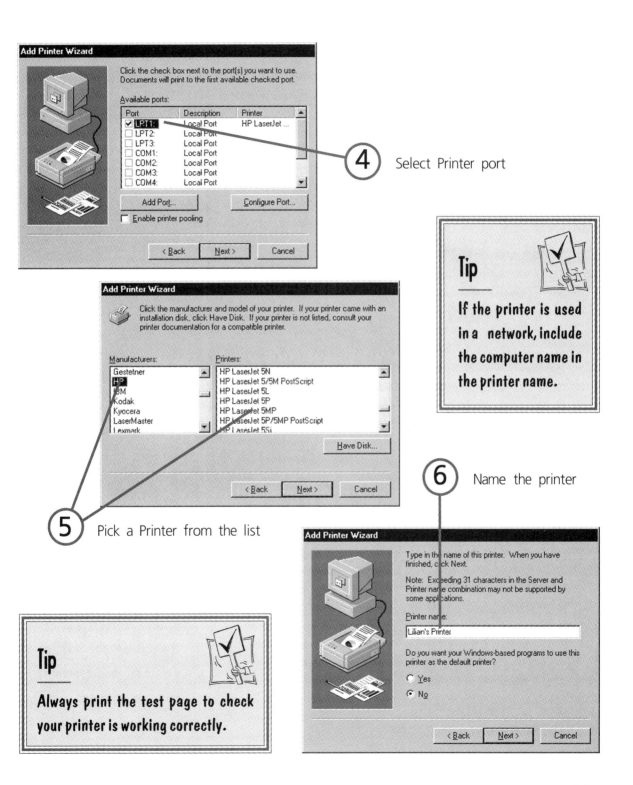

Add Printer Wizard

Click the check box next to the port(s) you want to use.
Documents will print to the first available checked port.

Available ports:

Port	Description	Printer
☑ LPT1:	Local Port	HP LaserJet ...
☐ LPT2:	Local Port	
☐ LPT3:	Local Port	
☐ COM1:	Local Port	
☐ COM2:	Local Port	
☐ COM3:	Local Port	
☐ COM4:	Local Port	

Add Port...   Configure Port...

☐ Enable printer pooling

< Back   Next >   Cancel

④ Select Printer port

Tip

If the printer is used
in a network, include
the computer name in
the printer name.

Add Printer Wizard

Click the manufacturer and model of your printer. If your printer came with an
installation disk, click Have Disk. If your printer is not listed, consult your
printer documentation for a compatible printer.

Manufacturers:

Gestetner
HP
IBM
Kodak
Kyocera
LaserMaster
Lexmark

Printers:

HP LaserJet 5N
HP LaserJet 5/5M PostScript
HP LaserJet 5L
HP LaserJet 5P
HP LaserJet 5MP
HP LaserJet 5P/5MP PostScript
HP LaserJet 5Si

Have Disk...

< Back   Next >   Cancel

⑤ Pick a Printer from the list

⑥ Name the printer

Tip

Always print the test page to check
your printer is working correctly.

Add Printer Wizard

Type in the name of this printer. When you have
finished, click Next.

Note: Exceeding 31 characters in the Server and
Printer name combination may not be supported by
some applications.

Printer name:

Lilian's Printer

Do you want your Windows-based programs to use this
printer as the default printer?

○ Yes
● No

< Back   Next >   Cancel

63

Default printer

Whenever anything is printed, the default printer is automatically used, unless the user specifies otherwise. If you only have one printer then there won't be any need to change this. Unfortunately you can't easily see which printer is the default until the properties are checked.

1 Click the icon in the **Control Panel**.

2 Click the icon for the printer.

3 Click **File**.

4 Click **Set as Default**.

(2) Select the printer

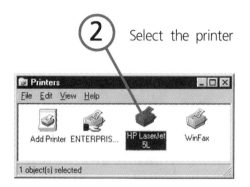

(3) Click on File

(4) Set this printer as the default

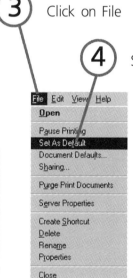

Take note

In this example the WinFax icon represents the fax machine, although it is really a modem that can send faxes. The computer treats it as a printer and it must be the default printer if you want to send a fax. Once the fax has been sent, set the default printer back to your normal printer.

Tip

From this drop down menu you can also perform other useful printer tasks, like pause the printer, share it and delete all the documents that it is printing.

Basic steps

1 Click on the 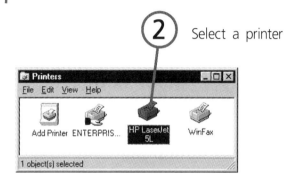 icon in
   Printers
   the Control Panel.

2 Click on the icon for
   the printer.

3 View the printer
   queue.

When a document is printing, unless it is a short one, you may want to know how much is left to print.

The printer queue will show the status of each document to be printed and the current state of the printer. Any actions such as pause the printer or stop printing a document, can be executed from the printer queue.

Tip

A faster route to obtain the printer queue, is to create a shortcut for the printer on the desktop. Double clicking on the desktop icon will display the printer queue.

(**2**) Select a printer

(**3**) Printer queue
To see more of the document name, pull this box to the right.

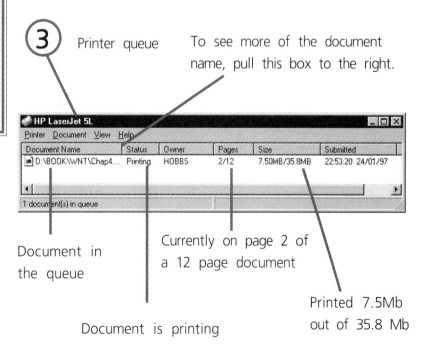

Document in
the queue

Currently on page 2 of
a 12 page document

Document is printing

Printed 7.5Mb
out of 35.8 Mb

Print me!

Despite living in the electronic age, paper is far from redundant, and the time has come to print a document.

Windows NT offers several ways to print. If you are within an application like Microsoft Word, then there is a printer icon to click or you can select Print from the File menu. Alternatively, you can do a quick print by dragging the document onto the printer icon on the desktop.

Printing is that easy. However, most printers contain special options, such as print in colour, use less toner, print graphics in high quality. These options will vary by printer and before you print you will given the option to select the ones that are appropriate.

❏ **Application**

1 Click on **File** then **Print**.

2 Check the default printer is correct.

3 Specify pages to print.

4 Specify number of pages to print.

5 Click on **Properties** to specify other options specific to this printer.

6 Click on **OK**.

7 Optionally check the printer queue to monitor progress.

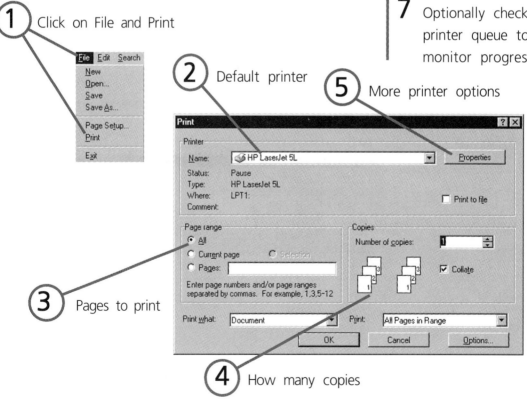

① Click on File and Print

② Default printer

⑤ More printer options

③ Pages to print

④ How many copies

Basic steps

❑ Quick print

8 Open the folder with the document to be printed.

9 Select the document.

10 Drag the document onto the printer icon on the desktop.

⑤ Printer options

Graphics resolution

Save toner?

Paper size?

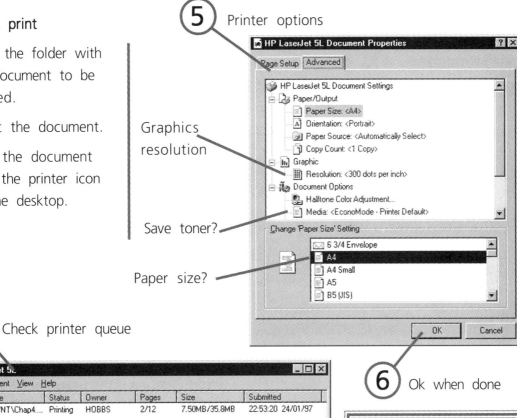

⑥ Ok when done

⑦ Check printer queue

⑧ Open the folder

⑨ Select the file

⑩ Drag to printer icon

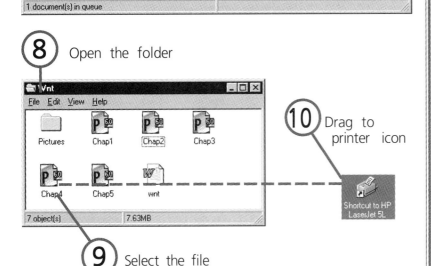

Tip

On some printers the document may not print immediately, especially if it contains pictures, so don't be surprised if there is a delay between requesting a document to print and when it first starts printing.

Please stop!

There will come a time, when you will look at the printer and wish it would stop. Perhaps the wrong document is being printed or you have accidentally asked it to print something and you want to delete it before it starts printing. Or maybe you just want to pause the printer and print later. All this can be achieved from the printer queue. From here you can stop either the printer or an individual document.

This is another good reason to have an icon on the desktop to get quickly to the printer queue display.

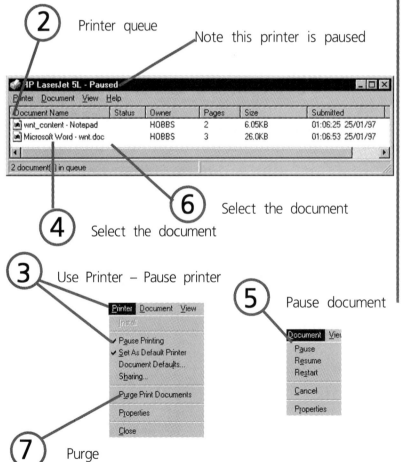

Printer queue

Note this printer is paused

Select the document

Select the document

Use Printer – Pause printer

Pause document

Purge

1 Click on the Printers icon in the Control Panel.

2 Select the printer and double click to display the printer queue.

❑ **Pause Printer**

3 From the **Printer** menu select **Pause printing**.

❑ **Pause Document**

4 Select document from the queue.

5 Open the **Document** menu and select **Pause**.

❑ **Delete Document**

6 Click on the document in the queue.

7 Click **Printer** then select **Purge Print Documents**.

or

8 Press the **Delete** key.

Basic steps

Share me!

1 Click on the Printers icon in the Control Panel.

2 Select the Printer.

3 Open the **Printer** menu and click on **Sharing**...

4 Select **Shared**.

5 Enter the name to identify the printer on the network.

6 Click on **OK**.

7 Check printer icon includes a hand. If not, return to step 3.

If you have more than one computer and they are connected together in a network, then you will want to share the printer so that all the computers can use it.

This is an important money saving tips because it means that you only have to own a limited number of printers.

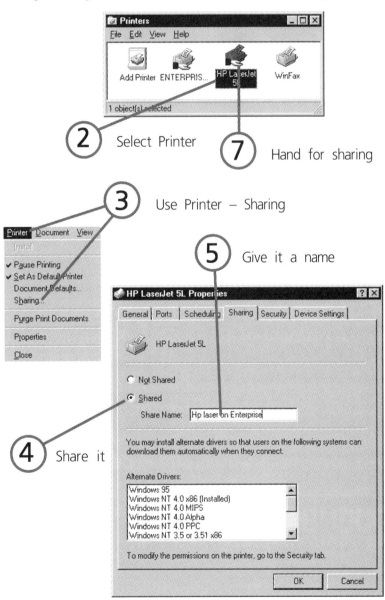

2 Select Printer

7 Hand for sharing

3 Use Printer — Sharing

5 Give it a name

4 Share it

Tip

It helps if the share name includes the computer name. Then it is easy to see to which computer the printer is attached.

69

Summary

- Each printer to be used must be set up using the **add printer wizard**.

- The **printer** specified as the **default** is used by all applications.

- Monitor the **print queue** to see the current state of printing.

- When printing don't forget to specify any **special options** like print 3 copies.

- Quickly print by *dragging* the document over a printer icon.

- **Pause** the printer to stop printing.

- **Delete** a document from the print queue using the delete key.

- The printer can be **shared** for use by all computers on the network.

6 System Management

Backup

When was the last time that you accidentally deleted a file or had a corrupt disk and needed to recover the files. It probably was quite a long time ago, but when it did happen, was it possible to recover the files?

If the deletion or corruption was recent, then you may have been able to use the Recycle Bin which is discussed later in this chapter. Chances are the Recycle Bin isn't sufficient and you will need to return to the last backup.

Now backups are very important, but it's amazing how many people don't bother to take them. NT provides the backup software so all that is required is a tape drive, as you cannot backup to disks. Tape drives are not that expensive today. They might seem an unnecessary expense, but it generally only takes one failure to prove their value. Many of us buy insurance to guard against something that hopefully will never happen. Backups are your computer insurance.

When selecting a tape drive, some important points to consider are how many megabytes a minute the tape can copy, how much data will fit on the tape and the price of the tape. For example, if a tape backups at the rate of 10mb per minute, then it is likely to take 100 minutes – over 1.5 hours – to backup one gigabyte!

Basic steps

1 Put a tape in the drive.

2 From the 🟦Start menu select **Programs**, then **Administrative Tools**, then **Backup**.

3 Select **Window**, then **Drives**. .

4 Select the **Drives** to backup. If you double click can select files to backup onto the disk.

5 Click on **Backup**.

6 Give the tape a name and the backup a description.

7 Click on OK to start the backup.

8 Monitor the progress of the backup.

9 When the backup has finished, remove the tape from the drive and store it safely.

> ## Tip
>
>
>
> To save tapes, one doesn't have to backup the entire disk. Instead select the important folders or files, because application software can always be reinstalled, although don't forget any configuration files that may have changed.

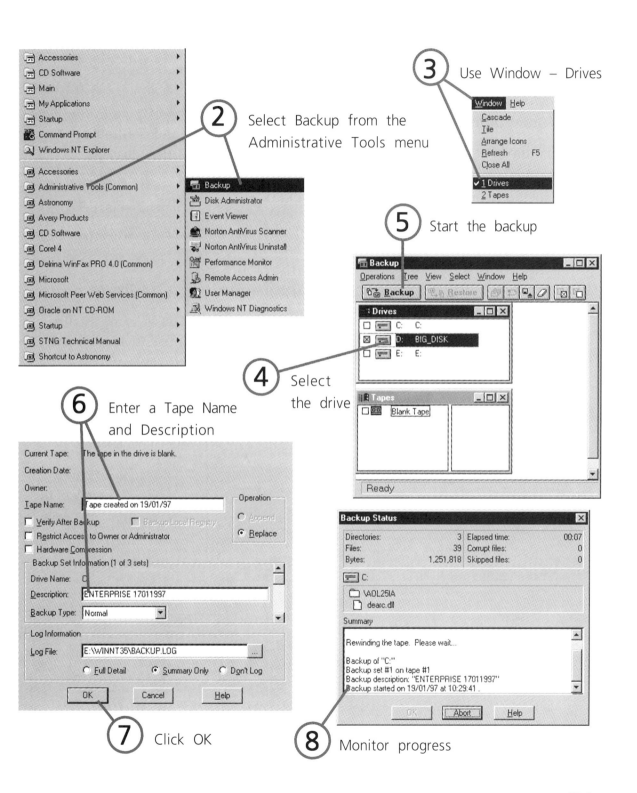

② Select Backup from the Administrative Tools menu

③ Use Window – Drives

⑤ Start the backup

④ Select the drive

⑥ Enter a Tape Name and Description

⑦ Click OK

⑧ Monitor progress

Restore

The moment has come that every computer user dreads, it is time to restore some files from a backup. If you have never restored files from a backup before don't worry, the restore utility is not hard to use.

One very important point to remember is that you can restore a single file from a backup. So if you lose that all–important file, head straight for the latest backup.

Whenever a backup is taken, write a helpful label, including the date, on the tape. If you are not sure what is on it, then the Restore utility will display all the files on the tape.

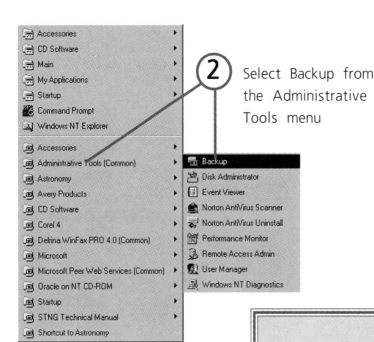

Select Backup from the Administrative Tools menu

1 Put a tape in the drive.

2 From the 🪟 Start menu select **Programs**, then **Administrative Tools**, then **Backup**.

3 From the **Window** menu select **Tapes**.

4 Click every folder or file or disk to restore.

5 Click **Restore**.

6 Specify where the files are to be restored.

7 Click **OK** to start the restore.

8 Monitor the progress of the restore.

9 When the restore has finished, remove the tape from the drive and return it to safe storage.

Tip

Before the tape is inserted into the drive, slide across the write protect switch to prevent accidental erase.

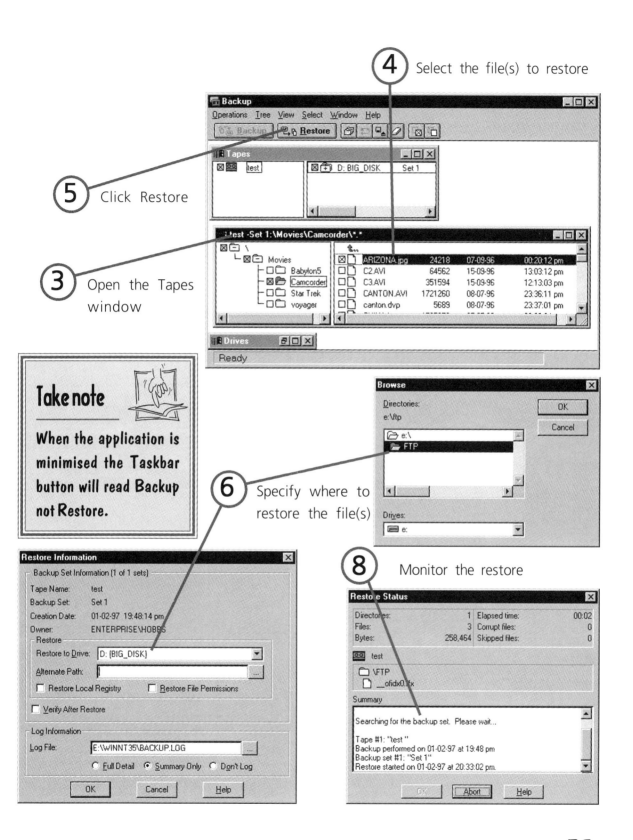

4 Select the file(s) to restore

5 Click Restore

3 Open the Tapes window

Take note

When the application is minimised the Taskbar button will read Backup not Restore.

6 Specify where to restore the file(s)

8 Monitor the restore

75

Event Viewer

There are three logs in NT where important events that occur on the computer are kept. They are:

- system log
- security log
- application log

The logs can be very useful when diagnosing problems, because they contain information about specific events and whether they were successful. The logs can be customised to record specific events and only those that result in a failure. There are quite a number of options available.

Basic steps

1 From the **Start** menu select **Programs** then **Administrative Tools** then **Event Viewer**.

2 Open the **Log** menu.

3 Select the type of log to be displayed.

4 From the **View** menu, select **Filter Events...**

5 Select the items to log and click on **OK**.

6 Click on any item for more detail.

(2) Click on Log

(3) Select the Application log

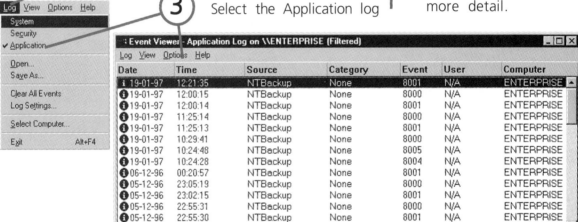

(4) Use View – Filter Events

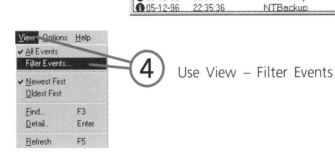

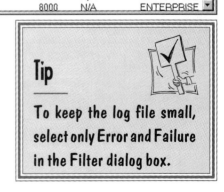

Tip

To keep the log file small, select only Error and Failure in the Filter dialog box.

Errors are shown as red icons

Time of error   Where error occurred

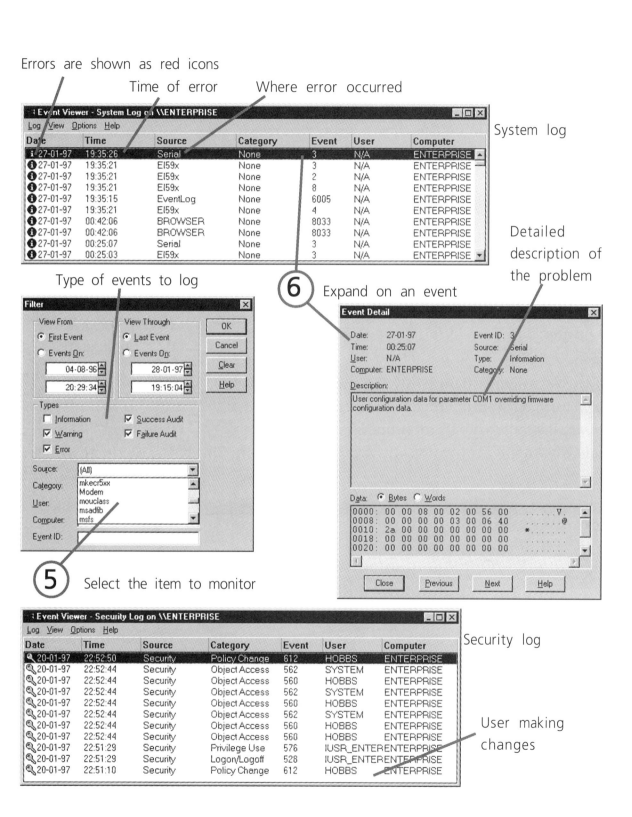

System log

Type of events to log

Detailed description of the problem

(6) Expand on an event

(5) Select the item to monitor

Security log

User making changes

Disk Administrator

Previous users of Windows will have managed their disks through the File Manager, now it must be done through the Disk Administrator. This can:

- Create volume and striped sets
- Format a disk
- Share a disk
- Setup security for the disk
- Create and delete disk partitions

This is mainly used with volume and striped sets, but it is nice to see graphically how full the disks are, using Disk Configuration view. New disks should be formatted using the Disk Administrator, not the MS-DOS Format command.

This Disk Administrator creates a harmless file, called a signature, on the disk. When NT asks if it may be created, agree. It is quite safe, even if your disk supports both NT and Windows 95.

Basic steps

1 From the **Start** menu select **Programs** then **Administrative Tools – Disk Administrator**.

2 If it is the first time Disk Administrator is run, confirm **Yes** to write the signature on the disk.

3 Click on **View** then choose **Volumes** or **Disk Configurations**.

4 Select an action from **Tools**.

5 Click on **Properties** to see details about the partition.

Disk Configuration view

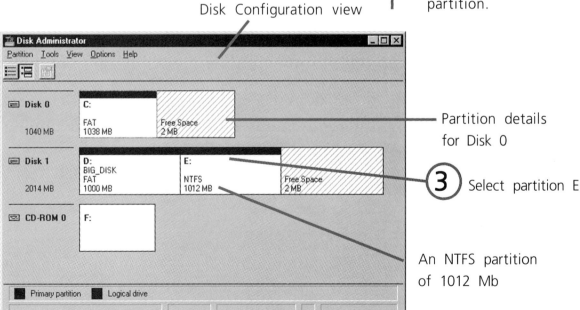

Partition details for Disk 0

(3) Select partition E

An NTFS partition of 1012 Mb

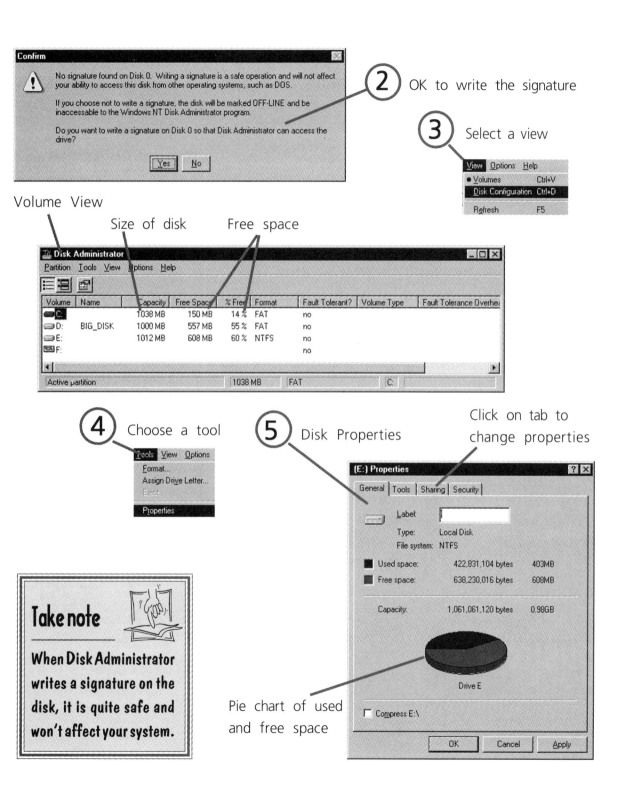

Confirm

No signature found on Disk 0. Writing a signature is a safe operation and will not affect your ability to access this disk from other operating systems, such as DOS.

If you choose not to write a signature, the disk will be marked OFF-LINE and be inaccessible to the Windows NT Disk Administrator program.

Do you want to write a signature on Disk 0 so that Disk Administrator can access the drive?

[Yes] [No]

(2) OK to write the signature

(3) Select a view

View Options Help
● Volumes   Ctrl+V
  Disk Configuration Ctrl+D
  Refresh   F5

Volume View

Size of disk   Free space

Disk Administrator

Partition Tools View Options Help

Volume	Name	Capacity	Free Space	% Free	Format	Fault Tolerant?	Volume Type	Fault Tolerance Overhead
C:		1038 MB	150 MB	14 %	FAT	no		
D:	BIG_DISK	1000 MB	557 MB	55 %	FAT	no		
E:		1012 MB	608 MB	60 %	NTFS	no		
F:						no		

Active partition   1038 MB   FAT   C:

(4) Choose a tool

Tools View Options
  Format...
  Assign Drive Letter...
  Eject

  Properties

(5) Disk Properties

Click on tab to change properties

(E:) Properties   ? ×

General | Tools | Sharing | Security |

Label:

Type: Local Disk
File system: NTFS

■ Used space: 422,831,104 bytes   403MB
■ Free space: 638,230,016 bytes   608MB

Capacity: 1,061,061,120 bytes   0.98GB

Drive E

☐ Compress E:\

[OK] [Cancel] [Apply]

Pie chart of used and free space

Take note

When Disk Administrator writes a signature on the disk, it is quite safe and won't affect your system.

Task manager

Windows NT can run multiple tasks at the same time which is good news for getting work done faster. The Task Manager allows you to monitor the performance of the system to see what resources each task is consuming and whether extra resources are required, like more memory.

Fortunately most of the information is displayed in a graphical form, so you don't have to be a computer expert to understand it.

As a general guide, if the CPU is constantly showing over 75%, a more powerful machine may be required.

The memory value used includes the physical memory plus the virtual memory disk. Ideally when the computer starts the memory in use should be less than the actual memory on the machine. e.g. this computer has 48Mb of memory and with some applications started, it is still using less than 38Mb.

Basic steps

1 Right click on any blank space on the taskbar and select **Task Manager**.

2 Check the CPU usage.

3 Check the memory usage.

4 Click on ☒ to finish.

① Select Task Manager

② CPU usage OK at 28%

Tip

Certain operations will consume high amounts of system resources. It is only when the computer is always near the maximum that purchase of extra resources should be considered.

③ Using less than 38Mb of memory

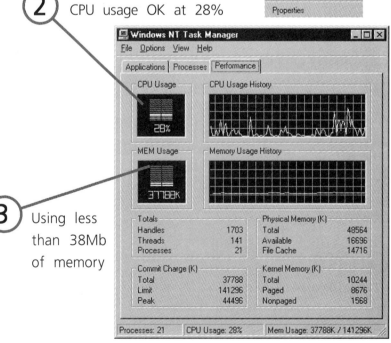

Task Manager — processes

1 Right click on any blank space on the taskbar and select **Task Manager**.

2 Open the **Processes** tab

3 Click on **View** then **Select Columns**.

4 Choose the columns to display.

5 Select a process and click [End Process] to stop it.

6 Click on any column head to sort by that value.

7 Click on ⊠ to finish.

The Task Manager also provides information on:

● applications running

● resources used by all processes

This information can be very useful when trying to determine which tasks are consuming all of the computer's resources.

Any application or task can be stopped from within the Task Manager, but take care not to delete something that NT needs to keep running. If you don't recognise the name of the task, don't delete it!

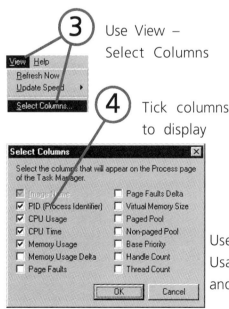

3 Use View – Select Columns

4 Tick columns to display

Useful ones are CPU Usage, CPU Time and Memory Usage

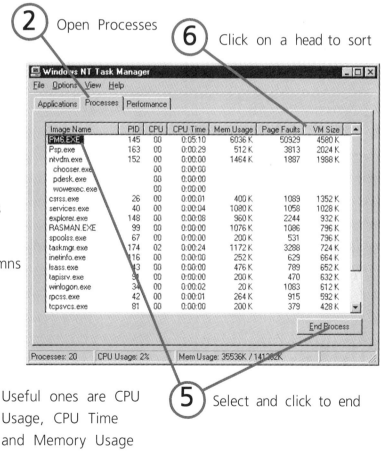

2 Open Processes

6 Click on a head to sort

5 Select and click to end

81

Stop that application

Sometimes applications do not behave as they should and need to be stopped. Two good methods for stopping an application are:

● from the Task Manager

● using [Ctrl] – [Alt] – [Delete] to invoke the Task Manager (see page 54).

This window cannot only be used for stopping an application. It can also be used to:

● switch to running another application

● start a new application, which is the equivalent of pressing the **Start** button.

1 Right click on any blank space on the Taskbar and select **Task Manager**.

or

1 Press [Ctrl] – [Alt] – [Delete], then select **Task Manager**.

2 Click on the **Applications** tab.

3 Select a process and click on End Task

4 Click on ⊠ to finish.

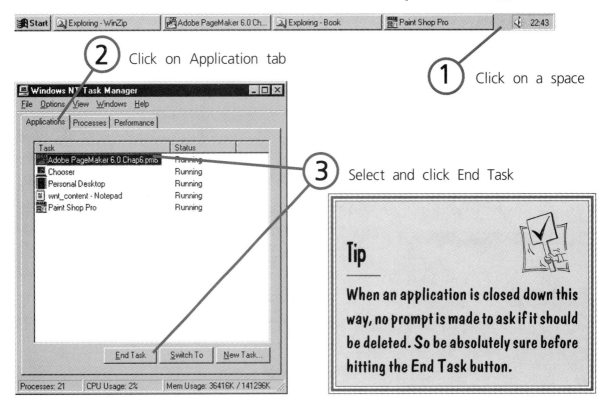

Click on Application tab

Click on a space

Select and click End Task

Tip

When an application is closed down this way, no prompt is made to ask if it should be deleted. So be absolutely sure before hitting the End Task button.

Basic steps

1
From the **Start** menu select **Programs** then **Administrative Tools** then **Performance Monitor**.

2
Click on **Edit** then select **Add to Chart**.

3
Select item to add to chart and press **Add**. Repeat for all items.

4
Click on ⊠ to finish.

5
Watch the chart.

Performance Monitor

Another tool that provides comprehensive information about system performance is the Performance Monitor. It should be said that unless you have a detailed knowledge of NT internals, the information you can understand from this scheme may be limited to a few resource items. Nevertheless, it is worth understanding how to collect data so that you can show it to an NT expert.

(2) Select Add to Chart

(3) Add this to the chart

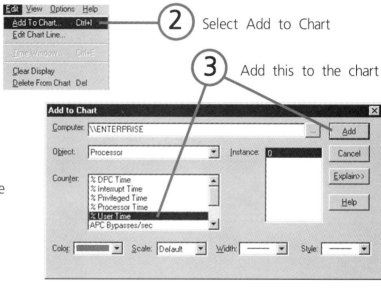

(1) Select the Performance Monitor

All the CPU was in use here

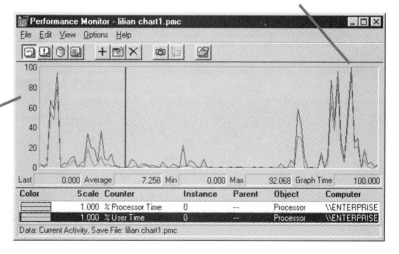

(5) Chart showing User time and Processor usage

Performance Monitor Log

We have already seen that the performance monitor can display a wealth of information, but many of us probably won't know how to interpret that information.

There is a log facility within the Performance Monitor which can be enabled at any time. You can specify the information that has to be collected. This is recorded in a file and can then be replayed as many times as necessary.

This file can then be given to an NT system expert for their opinion on system performance, therefore it is important to know how to collect the data that they require.

Basic steps

1 From the 🏁Start menu select **Programs** then **Administrative Tools** then **Performance Monitor**.

2 Click on **View** then **Log**.

3 Click on the **+** sign

4 Select item to add to log and press **Add**. Repeat for all items.

5 Click on **Done** to finish.

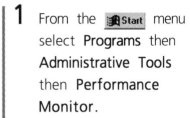

② Select View – Log

③ Click to add

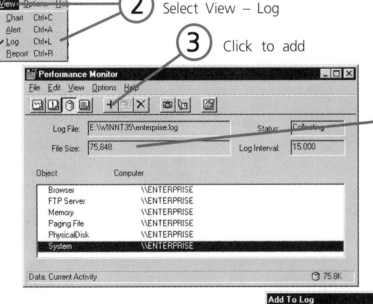

⑨ Size of log file

⑤ Done when all items added

④ Put this in log

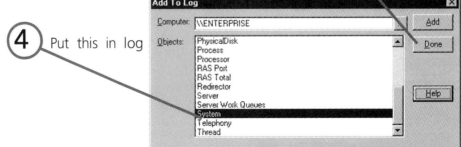

84

Basic steps

6 Click **Options** then **Log**.

7 Give the log file a name.

8 Click on **Start Log**.

9 Watch the size of the log file.

10 Click on **Stop log** to stop recording.

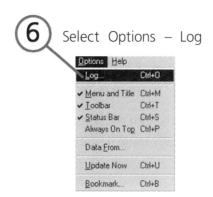

⑥ Select Options – Log

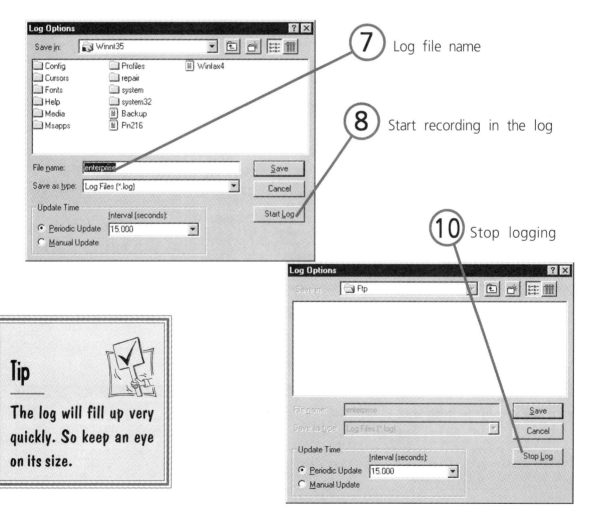

⑦ Log file name

⑧ Start recording in the log

⑩ Stop logging

Tip

The log will fill up very quickly. So keep an eye on its size.

Recycle Bin

The Recycle Bin is a new feature of NT V4.0 and it's very useful. How often have you deleted a file, program or document only to wish that you could retrieve it?

Everytime something is deleted it is placed in the Recycle Bin. Therefore it can be retrieved before the Recycle Bin is emptied. It is opened from an icon on the desktop and its contents are displayed.

The Recycle Bin should be monitored as part of routine system management. It should be emptied regularly, just like putting out the rubbish at home for the local council to collect!

② Items in the recycle bin

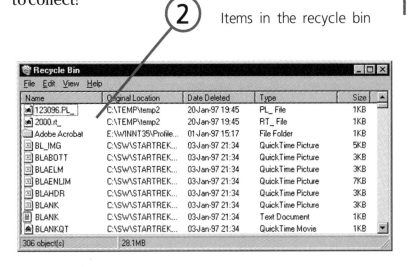

③ Empty bin

④ Confirm to empty the bin

Tip

If disk space is starting to run low then empty the Recycle Bin.

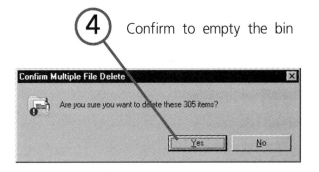

Basic steps

1 Click on the icon. Recycle Bin

2 Click on the heading to sort by this column.

3 Find the file to be restored from the recycle bin.

4 Click on **File** then **Restore**.

5 The file is now restored to its original location.

The Recycle Bin works just like a rubbish bin. A file or document can be tossed into the bin by the act of deleting, it can then be retrieved later.

So whenever you need to recover a file, first check the Recycle Bin. If it cannot be recovered from there then you will have to restore the file from a backup that was taken recently.

Restore this file

Click on these columns to sort

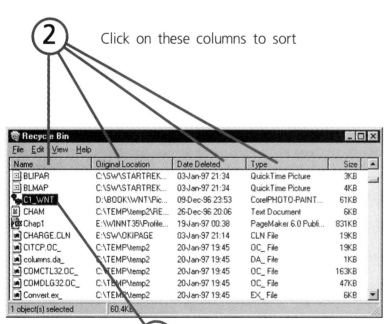

Select this file to restore

Tip

If the object that is to be restored cannot be seen in the list, check that this type of file has not been set to hidden in NT Explorer.

Summary

❑ Regularly use the **Backup** utility to take copies of important files on the computer.

❑ The NT backup utility **only** supports **tape** drives.

❑ Files can be recovered using the **Restore** option in the Backup utility.

❑ The **Event Viewer** displays information about security, applications and system events.

❑ The **Disk Administrator** should be used to format disks and create partitions.

❑ A disk can be **shared** using the Disk Administrator.

❑ View the amount of **free space** on a disk using the Disk Administrator.

❑ The **Task Manager** will show how the system is performing.

❑ A process or application can be **stopped** using the Task Manager.

❑ The **Performance Monitor** is another tool for showing system performance information.

❑ Resource information can be collected in the **Performance Monitor Log.**

❑ Regularly empty the **Recycle Bin.**

❑ Individual files can be **restored** from the Recycle Bin.

88

7 Networking

What is a Network

Most commercial computers are part of a **network** and you only need two computers to start one! A network could be a **LAN** or a **WAN**.

Networking computers is very important because it enables users to share their information, files, folders, applications and devices, such as printers, with other computer users.

Imagine the benefit of sharing a printer between 50 users, instead of having a printer for everyone or a place where documents are kept so that everyone shares them.

Joining a network is not compulsory, but it is wise to participate if one is present. Becoming part of the network does not mean that you have to share anything on your computer, but it does mean that you can take advantage of the network such as:

- use the corporate intranet or World Wide Web
- move files around easily between computers
- start sessions on other computers
- use one of the printers on the network

A computer cannot join the network unless it has a **network card** and a **network cable**. There are different types of cable connections and you should ask your network manager what type is in use. Unless you are on a specialist network, most network cards work with the popular protocols like Microsoft Network, TCP/IP and Netware.

The computer is connected to the network via the network card using a **network protocol**. The popular ones in use are:

- NETBEUI (page 92)
- TCP/IP (page 94)

Jargon

A **Network** is created when two or more computers are connected together and can exchange information.

LAN stands for Local Area Network. It is created when computers are networked using a high-speed cable. LANs are usually limited to a building or local site.

WAN stands for Wide Area Network. A good example would be a corporate network which spans the globe.

Network card is a card that is installed inside the computer.

Network cable is used to join the computer to the network. The cable is plugged into the network card.

Network protocol is a defined way of communicating with other computers.

Basic steps

1 Click the 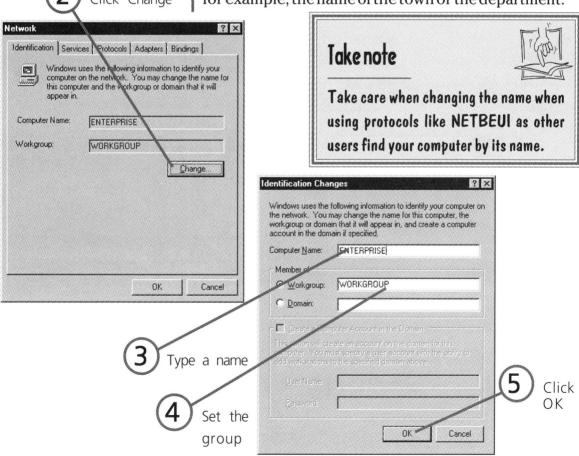 icon in
  the **Control Panel**.

2 Click **Change**.

3 Specify the name of
  the computer.

4 Specify the computer's
  workgroup.

5 Click on **OK**.

Name me!

Every computer on the network must have a name. In a small company it is not uncommon to find the computers named after cartoon characters or sci-fi shows. The only rule to abide by is that every name must be unique. In a corporate network, fun should be set aside and a practical naming convention used. For example, all PC's start with 'PC', mainframes with 'M' and mid-range systems with 'H'. If you define the naming convention wrong at the outset, changing it later may be impossible.

Workgroups – groups of computers on the network – are often named after the area where all the computers reside; for example, the name of the town or the department.

②　Click Change

Network

Identification | Services | Protocols | Adapters | Bindings

Windows uses the following information to identify your computer on the network. You may change the name for this computer and the workgroup or domain that it will appear in.

Computer Name: ENTERPRISE

Workgroup: WORKGROUP

[Change...]

[OK] [Cancel]

Take note

Take care when changing the name when using protocols like **NETBEUI** as other users find your computer by its name.

Identification Changes

Windows uses the following information to identify your computer on the network. You may change the name for this computer, the workgroup or domain that it will appear in, and create a computer account in the domain if specified.

Computer Name: ENTERPRISE

Member of
○ Workgroup: WORKGROUP
○ Domain:

☐ Create a Computer Account in the Domain

This option will create an account on the domain for this computer. You must specify a user account with the ability to add workstations to the specified domain above.

User Name:

Password:

[OK] [Cancel]

③　Type a name

④　Set the group

⑤　Click OK

Network setup

With the card installed in the computer, all of the desired network protocols must now be defined.

NETBEUI is the protocol around which Microsoft built the NT network architecture. It is a fast and efficient protocol and is ideal for small networks. The computer's name is used as the network address, therefore every computer on the network must have a unique name. As the number of computers increase, performance will degrade if the network consists of too many computers.

To communicate with existing Windows computers you will need to install NETBEUI. This is very straightforward, as NETBEUI requires no additional information.

1 Put the Windows NT 4 CD into the CD-ROM.

2 Click the 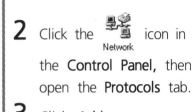 icon in the **Control Panel,** then open the **Protocols** tab.

3 Click **Add**

4 Select the Protocol and click **OK**.

5 Open the **Services** tab.

6 Click **Add** to select the service and click **OK**.

7 Open the **Adaptors** tab.

List of protocols already set up

(2) Protocols tab

(3) Add a new protocol

(4) Select NetBEUI and click OK

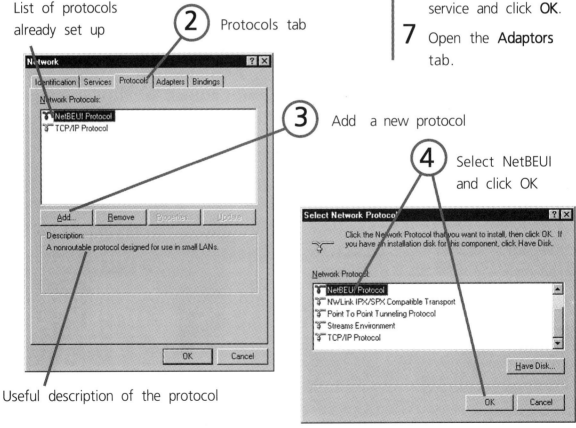

Useful description of the protocol

92

Basic steps

8 Find the name of your network card in the list.

9 If NT doesn't have the drivers then insert the floppy disk that came with the network card and click on **Have Disk**.

or

9 Click **OK**. The drivers will now be loaded.

10 Restart the computer to start the network.

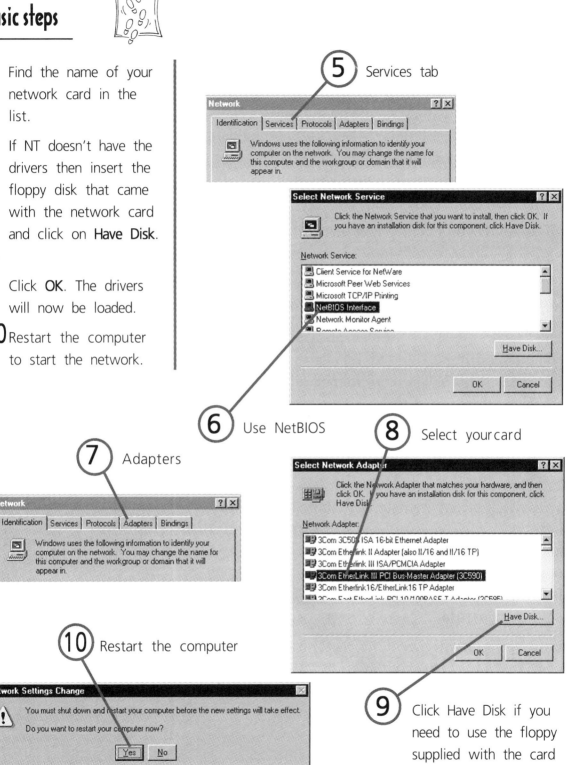

⑤ Services tab

⑥ Use NetBIOS

⑦ Adapters

⑧ Select your card

⑨ Click Have Disk if you need to use the floppy supplied with the card

⑩ Restart the computer

93

TCP/IP

TCP/IP must be installed if the computer will be connected to the Internet or operating systems like Unix or OpenVMS. It is ideal to use on complex, wide area networks and is used widely in the computer industry. It provides an efficient mechanism to connect to other computers on the network and for copying files between computers.

All computers on a TCP/IP network will be allocated:

- Computer name
- IP Address
- Subnet mask

The **IP address** will take the form of xx.xx.xx.xx and every computer on the network has a similar address. A typical address is 10.45.7.104 which is allocated by the network administrator.

The **subnet mask** is a number similar to the IP address and you will told the value for your site by the network administrator.

These three basic parameters are sufficient to join a TCP/IP network, but there are several other parameters that are also useful.

- IP address of **gateway** computer
- Optional IP address of **DNS** server
- Optional IP address of **WINS** server

Don't worry if you are reading this and thinking, I will never remember these computers by their numbers. Help is at hand so you can call the computer ENTERPRISE instead of 138.3.8.19

Jargon

TCP/IP stands for Transmission Control Protocol/Internet Protocol

Computer name is a unique name for the computer.

IP address is the number given to the computer to uniquely identify it on the network.

Subnet mask is a number similar to the IP address, often of the form 255.255.255.0

Gateway is the IP address of the computer on the network from which you can reach computers outside of your network group.

DNS stands for Domain Name System. It translates names into IP addresses.

WINS stands for Windows Internet Name Service. It is another service for translating names into IP addresses.

Basic steps

1 Put the Windows NT 4 CD into the CD-ROM.

2 Follow the steps on page 94 for setting up a network protocol.

3 Specify the TCP/IP parameters.

4 Click **OK** then restart the computer.

5 Ping another computer to verify network connection.

IP address tab

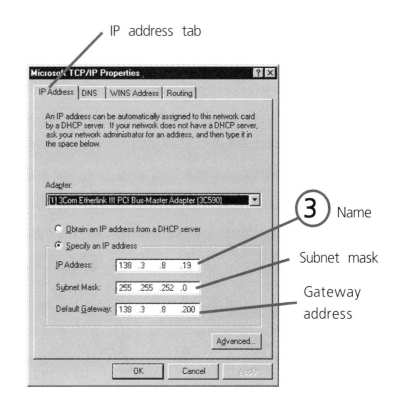

③ Name

Subnet mask

Gateway address

Tip

To test the network connection, run the application ping with an IP address. If the remote computer responds, you are on the network.

⑤ Test network connection

Remote computer is responding

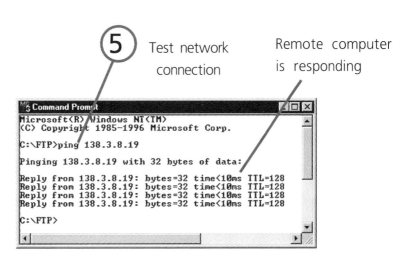

Sharing folders

Now that the computer is on the network it is time to share your files and folders with other users on the network.

Don't worry about people snooping around your private files – no one has access to any of your files or folders unless you grant them permission.

The security provide by NT is quite sophisticated – for every folder or document or application you can specify:

● which users may access

● how those users can access (NTFS disks only)

Therefore you could allow everyone access to your folders, but only for reading. Alternatively, all users could read and the HOBBS user could update.

Basic steps

1 Click on the icon

2 Locate the folder to be shared.

3 Click on **File** then **Properties**.

4 Open the **Sharing** tab.

5 Enter the share name and a comment.

6 Click on **Permissions**.

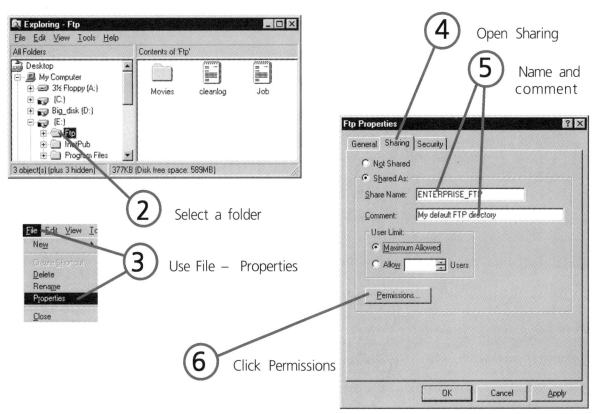

④ Open Sharing

⑤ Name and comment

② Select a folder

③ Use File – Properties

⑥ Click Permissions

Basic steps

7 Click on **Add**.

8 Select a user or group.

9 Select type of access.

10 Click **Add** to add to those authorised to access the folder

11 Click **OK**.

12 Check that folder is now shared.

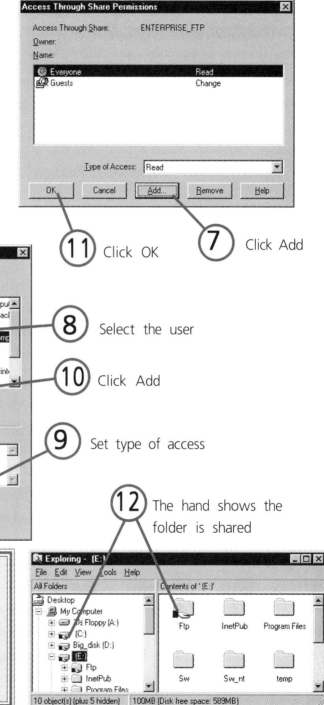

11 Click OK

7 Click Add

8 Select the user

10 Click Add

9 Set type of access

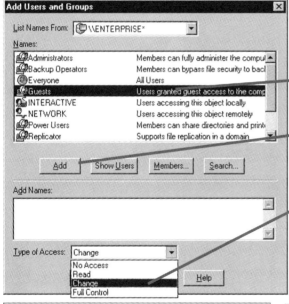

12 The hand shows the folder is shared

Secure that file

So far we have seen how to specify who can look at files and folders on our computer. Now it is time to specify which actions the user may perform against our files.

If the disk has been formatted as NTFS then for every file we can specify whether a visitor is allowed to:

- read
- change
- full access
- no access
- special access combination of read, write, execute, delete and take ownership

At any time the file permissions can be changed and they take effect immediately. In addition if you are concerned about unauthorised access to specific files, then an audit log can be enabled to report any unauthorised access attempts.

Basic steps

1 Start **Explorer**.

2 Find the file to be secured and click the right mouse button.

3 Click **Properties**.

4 Click **Permissions**.

5 Select the users and access rights.

6 Click **Add**.

7 Optionally click on **Special Access**.

8 Select access rights and click **OK**..

9 Check the access rights screen for each user and group and click **OK**.

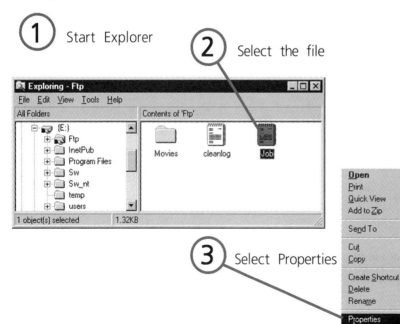

① Start Explorer

② Select the file

③ Select Properties

Tip

If strict individual file security is required then disks must be formatted as NTFS.

98

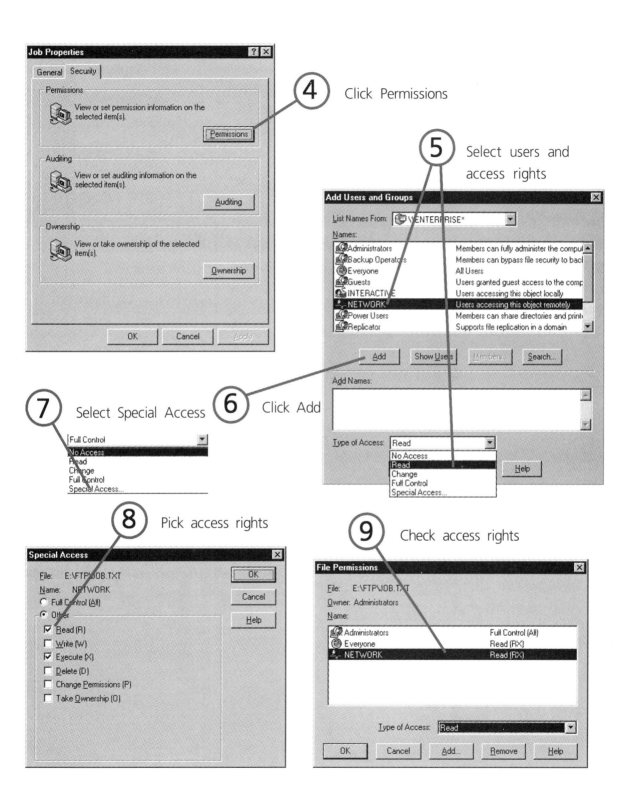

Job Properties

General | Security

Permissions
View or set permission information on the selected item(s).
[Permissions]

④ Click Permissions

Auditing
View or set auditing information on the selected item(s).
[Auditing]

Ownership
View or take ownership of the selected item(s).
[Ownership]

[OK] [Cancel] [Apply]

⑤ Select users and access rights

Add Users and Groups

List Names From: [🖳\\ENTERPRISE*]

Names:
Administrators	Members can fully administer the compu
Backup Operators	Members can bypass file security to bacl
Everyone	All Users
Guests	Users granted guest access to the comp
INTERACTIVE	Users accessing this object locally
NETWORK	Users accessing this object remotely
Power Users	Members can share directories and print
Replicator	Supports file replication in a domain

[Add] [Show Users] [Members...] [Search...]

Add Names:

Type of Access: [Read]

No Access
Read
Change
Full Control
Special Access...

[Help]

⑦ Select Special Access

Full Control
No Access
Read
Change
Full Control
Special Access...

⑥ Click Add

⑧ Pick access rights

Special Access

File: E:\FTP\JOB.TXT
Name: NETWORK
○ Full Control (All)
● Other
☑ Read (R)
☐ Write (W)
☑ Execute (X)
☐ Delete (D)
☐ Change Permissions (P)
☐ Take Ownership (O)

[OK] [Cancel] [Help]

⑨ Check access rights

File Permissions

File: E:\FTP\JOB.TXT
Owner: Administrators
Name:
Administrators	Full Control (All)
Everyone	Read (RX)
NETWORK	Read (RX)

Type of Access: [Read]

[OK] [Cancel] [Add...] [Remove] [Help]

99

Who is out there?

Okay, so we have connected our computer to the network, decided to share some of our folders with other network users, but how do we know who else is on the network. There are several ways we can find out:

- Windows NT Explorer

- Network neighbourhood

Since it is quite likely that NT Explorer is already active, this is usually the fastest way to see the computers on the network. One of the problems with using the network neighbourhood icon, is that it normally creates a new window each time you select. Hold [Ctrl] down as you select the next level, and it will open in the same window.

Basic steps

1 Start **Explorer**.

2 Click **Network Neighborhood**.

3 Expand the hierarchy by clicking on **Microsoft Windows Network**.

4 Choose a group to expand.

5 Pick a computer from the list.

6 See the folders available.

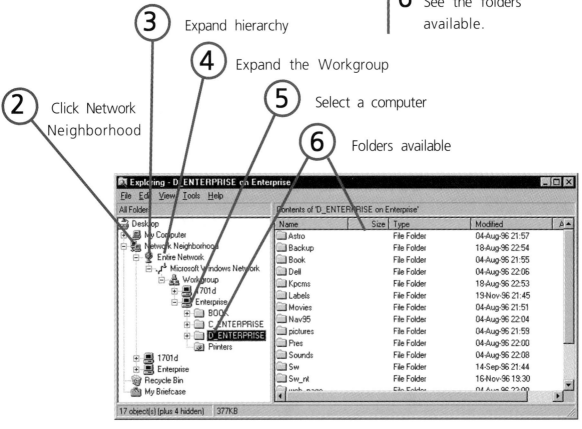

③ Expand hierarchy

④ Expand the Workgroup

② Click Network Neighborhood

⑤ Select a computer

⑥ Folders available

Basic steps

1 Click on the [Network Neighborhood] icon

2 Click **Entire Network**.

3 Double click on **Microsoft Windows Networking**.

4 Click on **Workgroup** or group name.

5 Pick a computer and click to expand what is available.

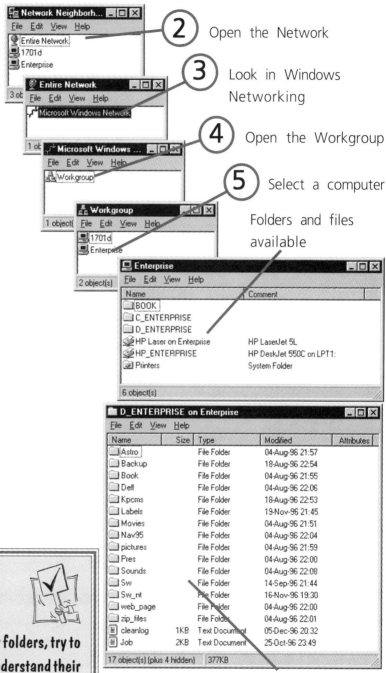

② Open the Network

③ Look in Windows Networking

④ Open the Workgroup

⑤ Select a computer

Folders and files available

Contents of the D disk on the computer called Enterprise

Tip

When the computer is first switched on, not all the computers on the network may appear immediately. Wait a few minutes and they should all be visible.

Tip

If you plan to share your files or folders, try to name them so other users can understand their contents, e.g. *April Newsletter.*

Mapping network drives

Basic steps

We have spent most of this chapter learning how to connect to the network and sharing our files with other users. Now it is time to reverse the roles, and connect to a remote computer and look at somebody else's files.

When you connect to a disk on a remote computer, NT allocates that disk a letter, so that it looks and behaves just like a disk that is connected to your own computer. You can drag and drop files and folders in Explorer, and access the remote computer as a drive from within applications.

There is also no need to worry about trying to remember the name of the remote computer, because NT will display a list of all the visible computers. However, if the computer that you want to connect to is not in the list, you can still type its name and NT will find it on the network.

Whenever a connection to a remote computer is made, NT will ask whether this connection should be automatically made the next time you logon.

1 Start **Explorer**.

2 Click on **Tools** then **Map Network Drive**.

3 Expand the hierarchy by clicking on **Microsoft Windows Network**.

4 Choose a group to expand.

5 Pick a computer from the list and click to expand what is available.

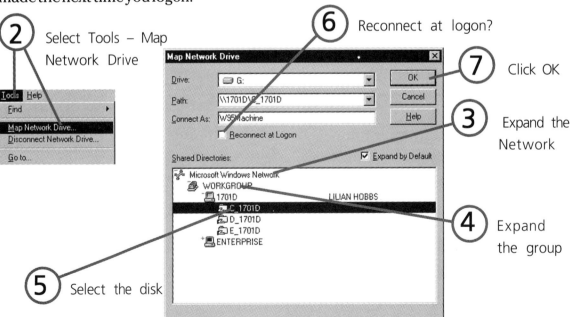

② Select Tools – Map Network Drive

⑥ Reconnect at logon?

⑦ Click OK

③ Expand the Network

④ Expand the group

⑤ Select the disk

Basic steps

6 Click on **Reconnect at logon** to automatically reconnect to the network drive when you next logon.

7 Click **OK** to finish.

8 The r emote disk is now available.

9 Repeat stpes 2 to 7 to connect to more remote computers.

Tip

Connections to remote computers can automatically be re-established every time the computer is started, by clicking on the Reconnect at logon box when the connection is first defined.

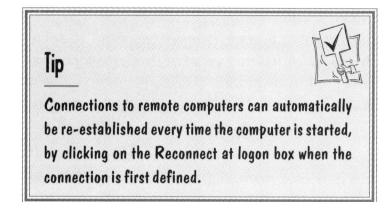

⑦ Remote disk is available as the disk G

⑧ Now connected to two remote disks

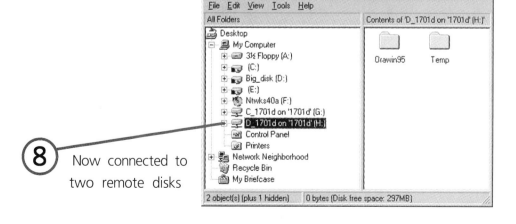

Anybody out there?

Traditionally computer users are not used to sharing their personal computer with other users. NT has changed that, because it is now very easy to share your disks and folders with other users. Therefore before you switch off your computer or stop sharing a disk, first you must check to see if anyone is using your computer.

If people are using your computer, you have the ability to disconnect them from it. However, it is best to contact them first and ask if you can disconnect them. Otherwise, the files they are working on may be lost or become corrupt if your disk is suddenly no longer available.

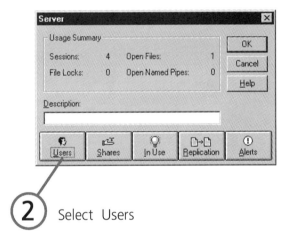

(2) Select Users

Take note

Don't share disks and folders if you plan to regularly switch off your computer because you may spend too much time contacting connected users.

1 Click on the Server icon in the **Control Panel**.

2 Click on the **Users** button.

3 See if there are any users connected to your computer.

4 See which shared resources other users have open.

5 Contact the users to confirm that no work will be lost when the link to your computer is removed.

6 Click on **Disconnect All** to remove all users from this computer.

7 Click on **Yes** to confirm their removal.

8 Verify that all users have been removed.

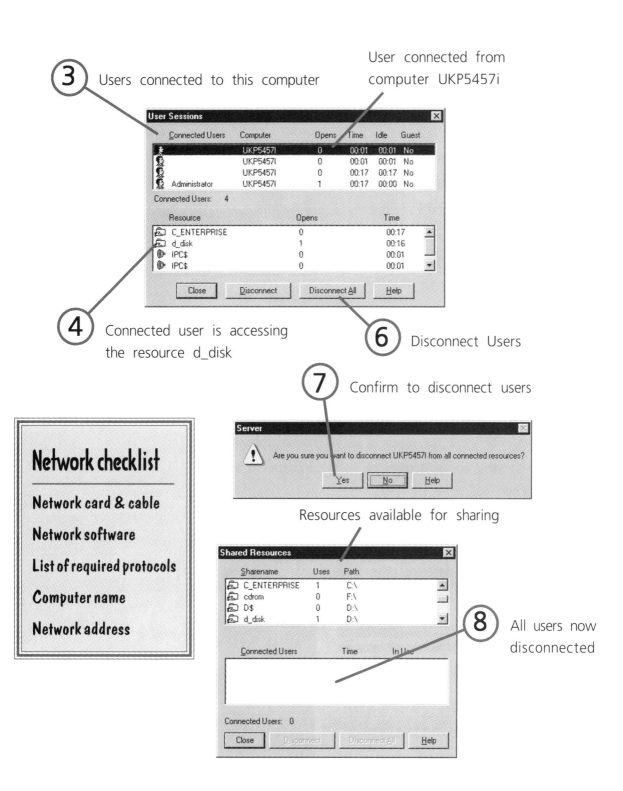

③ Users connected to this computer

User connected from computer UKP5457i

User Sessions

Connected Users	Computer	Opens	Time	Idle	Guest
	UKP5457I	0	00:01	00:01	No
	UKP5457I	0	00:01	00:01	No
	UKP5457I	0	00:17	00:17	No
Administrator	UKP5457I	1	00:17	00:00	No

Connected Users: 4

Resource	Opens	Time
C_ENTERPRISE	0	00:17
d_disk	1	00:16
IPC$	0	00:01
IPC$	0	00:01

Close   Disconnect   Disconnect All   Help

④ Connected user is accessing the resource d_disk

⑥ Disconnect Users

⑦ Confirm to disconnect users

Network checklist

Network card & cable

Network software

List of required protocols

Computer name

Network address

Server

⚠ Are you sure you want to disconnect UKP5457I from all connected resources?

Yes   No   Help

Resources available for sharing

Shared Resources

Sharename	Uses	Path
C_ENTERPRISE	1	C:\
cdrom	0	F:\
D$	0	D:\
d_disk	1	D:\

⑧ All users now disconnected

Connected Users	Time	In Use

Connected Users: 0

Close   Disconnect   Disconnect All   Help

105

Summary

- A **network** is created when two or more computers are joined together.

- The computers are connected using a **network protocol**.

- A **network card** is required to attach the computer to a network.

- Every computer on the network must have a unique **computer name.**

- Use the **NETBEUI** to connect to computers using Windows for Workgroups, Windows 95 or Windows NT.

- **TCP/IP** is the protocol to use if the computer is going to be connected to a large network.

- **TCP/IP** is used by computers on the Internet.

- Folders can be **shared** to allow specific computer users access to them.

- Users may only **access folders** or files using the methods granted to them.

- From within **NT Explorer** you can see all the computers on the network.

- Using the **map to network drive** a user can connect to disks on remote computers.

- Use the **Server** to check if anyone is connected to your computer before shutting down.

8 Networking tools

WINS

Now that the computer is connected to the network, we need to be able to easily find all the other computers on the network.

Windows Internet Naming Service known as WINS maps IP addresses to NETBIOS or NETBEUI computer names. The advantage of using the WINS server is that you don't have to keep your own list of computer names and their IP addresses. Instead you call the WINS server and obtain the very latest information. Fortunately this does not mean that the computer will run slower, so using a WINS server makes good sense.

Not every site uses WINS so you will have to ask your network administrator if it is available.

1 Click the 🖥️ icon in the Control Panel.

2 Open the **Protocols** tab.

3 Double click on the **TCP/IP service**.

4 Open the **WINS** tab.

5 Enter the IP address of the WINS server.

6 Click **OK** and restart the computer.

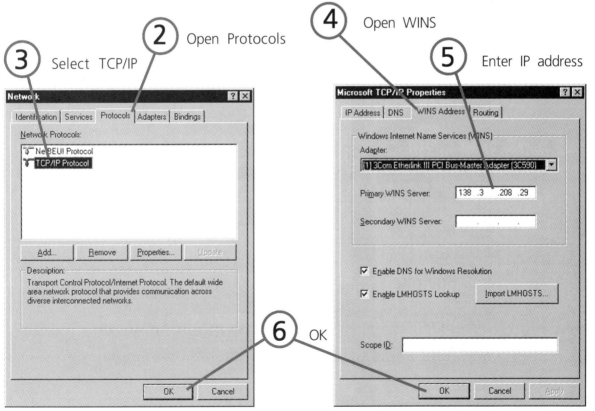

③ Select TCP/IP

② Open Protocols

④ Open WINS

⑤ Enter IP address

⑥ OK

Basic steps

1 Click the icon in the Control Oanel.

2 Open the **Protocols** tab.

3 Double click on the **TCP/IP service**.

4 Click on the **DNS** tab.

5 Click **Add**.

6 Enter the IP address of the DNS server.

7 Click **OK** and restart the computer.

Another method for resolving IP addresses to computer names is to use the Domain Name Service (DNS). This maps computer's names to IP addresses for people using the TCP/IP service.

At first glance it looks identical to the WINS service, but it does more because it translate names like www.oracle.com to the computer hosting that Web site.

Fortunately, you don't have to worry about how to setup a DNS service. All you need to do is ask your network administrator the IP addresses of the machines providing the DNS service and you are done!

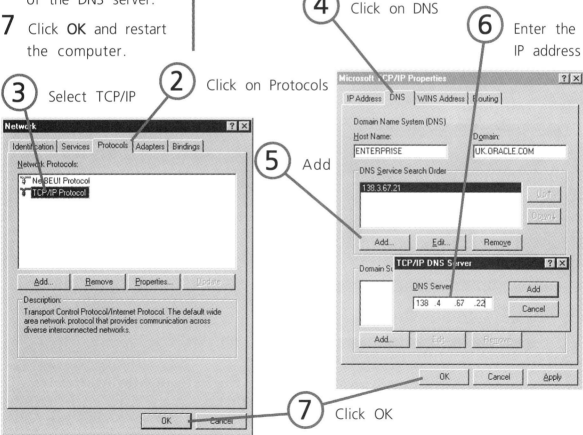

(4) Click on DNS

(6) Enter the IP address

(2) Click on Protocols

(3) Select TCP/IP

(5) Add

(7) Click OK

Ping

When you participate in a network, one of the first things you want to do is test whether your are properly connected. Unfortunately, NT won't always tell you that the network isn't working. Therefore, you try to attach to a remote computer and you sit there and wait. Now you ask yourself, is it taking a long time because the network isn't working or because there is a delay on the network.

The answer to the question is to run a simple little program called **ping**. You can either give ping the IP address or the name of the computer that you are trying to reach. Ping will then instantly tell you whether it reached the computer and if so how long it took. On NT it will poll the remote computer three times and then stop, so don't look away or you will miss it!

Basic steps

1 Click **Start** then click on **Run**.

2 Enter **ping** and the IP address or the computer name.

3 *Timed out* means that the network failed.

4 A response means that the network is working.

(4) This computer is reachable

(2) Type ping and the name or address

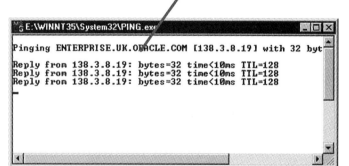

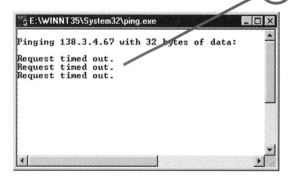

(3) This computer is off-line

Tip

First try ping with the IP address to see if the network is working correctly.

110

Basic steps

1 Click then click on **Run**.

2 Enter **telnet** and the IP address or the computer name.

3 Start a session on the remote computer.

There is another very useful utility supplied with NT called **telnet** which allows you to log on to another computer. Telnet would be used to connect to a computer running another operating system like Unix or OpenVMS.

Typical users of this utility are people on a corporate network who need to access the larger computers within the organisation.

This isn't a very sophisticated terminal emulation application but it does provide basic facilities. Therefore it's quite likely that if you have to access non-NT computers frequently, you will find another application for this job.

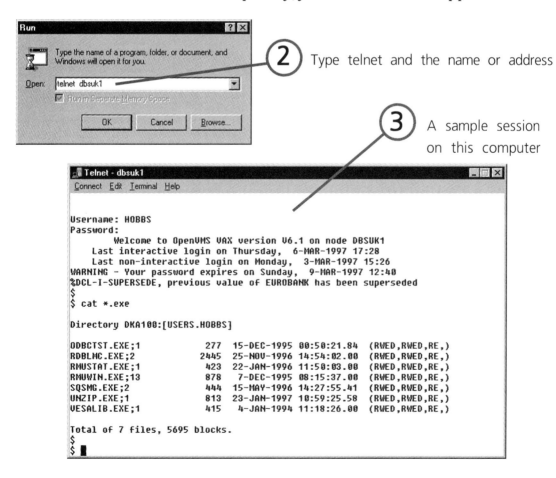

(**2**) Type telnet and the name or address

(**3**) A sample session on this computer

Workgroup

One of the parameters required when the network is setup, is the workgroup of each computer. A workgroup represents a collection of computers. One advantage of workgroups, is that when the Network Neighborhood is displayed, the first level of the hierarchy is the workgroup.

The workgroup is a logical concept. It can be very useful. Suppose a company has 100 NT computers, located in 5 offices around the country. A workgroup is created for each office and each computer in that office is assigned to that workgroup. It is then easy to see where a computer is located.

Workgroups can be changed at any time, but it is a good idea to develop a naming convention and stick to it.

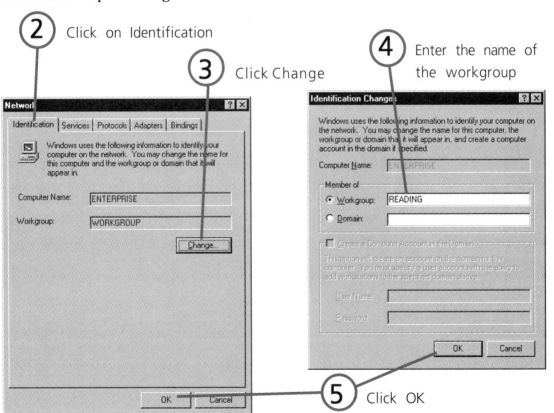

(2) Click on Identification

(3) Click Change

(4) Enter the name of the workgroup

(5) Click OK

1 Locate the file called **hosts** or **lmhosts** in the folder where NT is installed in **\system32\drivers\etc**

2 Open the file using the **Notepad** or other editing tool.

3 Edit the file to include the TCP/IP address and the computer name.

4 Save the file, ensuring that it does not have a file extension. The network software will automatically use it the next time the network is used.

We have already seen that on a corporate network, the addresses of other computers can be found by using the WINS or DNS server. But what if your computer is on a small network that doesn't have any of these services, how do you locate another computer?

NT will contact each of the computers on the network to establish its identify but there is faster method, if you are using the TCP/IP protocol, to create a file called:

● LMHOSTS to translate NetBIOS names to TCP/IP address

● HOSTS to translate TCP/IP addresses to an NT computer name

NT provides sample files, with a file extension of .SAM, which can be found in \system32\drivers\etc in the folder where the NT software is installed. Edit them to include the computer name and TCP/IP address and save *without a file extension*. Therefore the file **hosts.sam** becomes **hosts**.

The main disadvantage of this approach is that every time a new computer is added to the network, the file on every computer must be edited. This technique should only be used on very small networks, or to keep a quick lookup of addresses for computers that you access regularly.

```
# This is a  HOSTS file used by TCP/IP for Windows NT.
#
127.0.0.1     localhost
138.3.8.19    ENTERPRISE
130.3.8.20    VOYAGER
```

3 Enter the TCP/IP address and the computer name

Dial-in to a network

Some of us will need to dial-in to a remote computer. This could be the method used to connect to our Internet provider or to connect to an employer's computer system.

Whatever your reason, a wizard is provided to simplify the job of creating the connection. Some Internet providers will do all this work for you, but it is good idea to know how to set it up yourself.

(3) Click on New

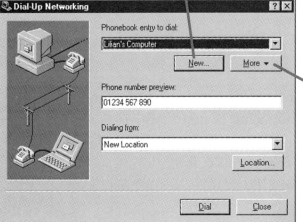

(8) Click on more

(4)   Name for the connection

(5)   Set the options

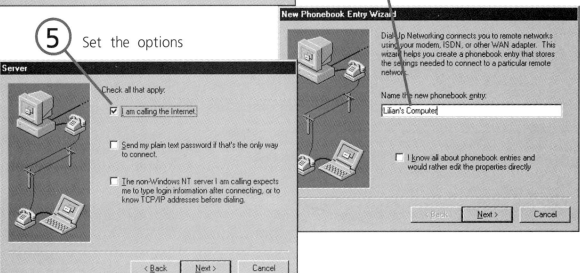

Basic steps

6 Enter the telephone number and click **Next**.

7 Click **Finish**.

8 Back at the Dial-Up Networking dialog box, click **More**.

9 Select create a shortcut

10 Name the shortcut and click **OK**.

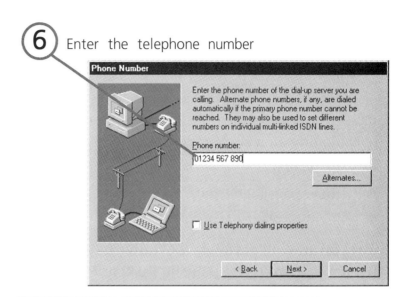

(6) Enter the telephone number

Phone Number

Enter the phone number of the dial-up server you are calling. Alternate phone numbers, if any, are dialed automatically if the primary phone number cannot be reached. They may also be used to set different numbers on individual multi-linked ISDN lines.

Phone number:
01234 567 890

Alternates...

☐ Use Telephony dialing properties

< Back   Next >   Cancel

(9) Create a shortcut

Edit entry and modem properties...
Clone entry and modem properties...
Delete entry...
Create shortcut to entry...

Monitor status...

Operator assisted or manual dialing
User preferences...
Logon preferences...

Help

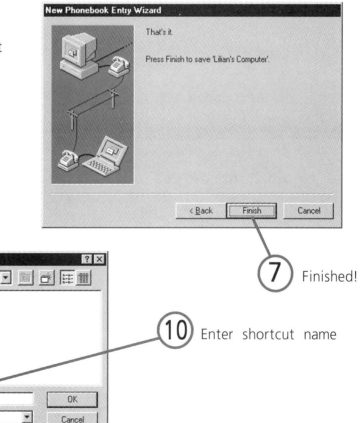

New Phonebook Entry Wizard

That's it.

Press Finish to save 'Lilian's Computer'.

< Back   Finish   Cancel

(7) Finished!

(10) Enter shortcut name

Create Dial-Up Shortcut   ? ✕

Look in: 📑 Desktop

🖳 My Computer
🖳 Network Neighborhood
📇 My Briefcase
📄 ClaraNet
📄 Shortcut to Wnt

File name: Lilian's Computer   OK

Files of type: Dial-up shortcut files (*.rnk)   Cancel

Dial-up monitor

When you are connected to a remote computer, Windows NT provides a very useful tool to monitor your connection. The dial-up monitor provides a wealth of information, most of it probably falls into the nice-to-know category, like how much data has been received. However, there is some very useful information, so check out:

- line speed
- time spent connected
- location of the hangup button

The Dial-up Monitor can also be started by clicking on the telephone icon ⟨ ⟩ 23:31 on the Taskbar.

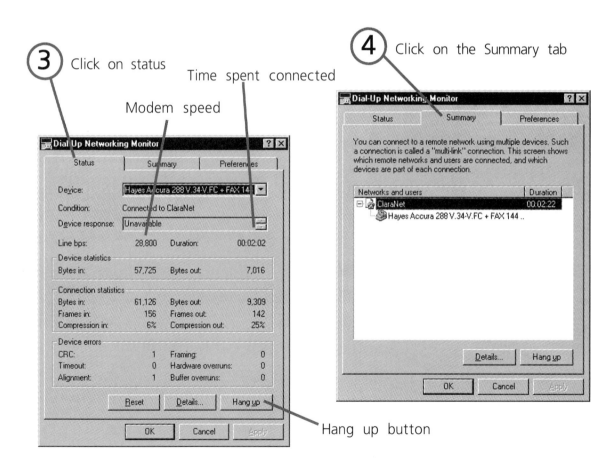

③ Click on status

Time spent connected

Modem speed

④ Click on the Summary tab

Hang up button

Modem

1 Click on the  **Modems** icon in the Control Panel.

2 Select the modem.

3 Click on **properties**.

4 Set the **Speaker Volume**.

5 Set the **Maximum Speed**.

6 Click on **OK**.

Setting up a modem couldn't be easier with Windows NT. No longer is it necessary to try and remember those horrid modem codes like ATD0. Now the modem is configured from the Modem Properties dialog box by clicking on the required attributes.

NT can be configured to support several modems, but most of us will only have one. The general screen identifies our modem and will tell us how long we have been connected.

Selecting the modem and then click on properties, useful attributes can be set, like the volume of the modem speaker and its maximum speed.

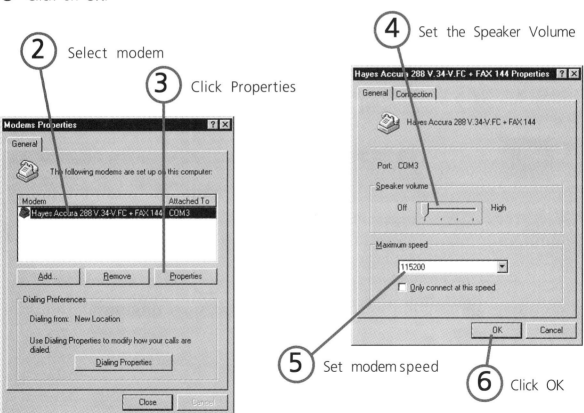

(2) Select modem

(3) Click Properties

(4) Set the Speaker Volume

(5) Set modem speed

(6) Click OK

Briefcase

How many times have you had a file on your computer, transferred it to another computer, and then not been sure if you copied it back to the computer where it originally came from. If this sounds like a familiar story then what you need is the Windows NT Briefcase.

The Briefcase is automatically installed and allows you to remove files from your computer, work on them elsewhere, return to your computer and then update the versions on your computer.

The secret to using the Briefcase is to think about it as a real briefcase. So whenever you use it, imagine collecting your files, put them in the briefcase and take it with you.

One nice feature of the Briefcase is that it can be used to transfer files either to a floppy disk, or to another computer or laptop on the network.

Basic steps

1 Double click on the icon on the desktop.

2 Drag the document onto the Briefcase.

3 Close the Briefcase.

4 Drag the contents of the Briefcase or the file to the floppy disk or the Briefcase on the other computer.

5 Make the changes to the document.

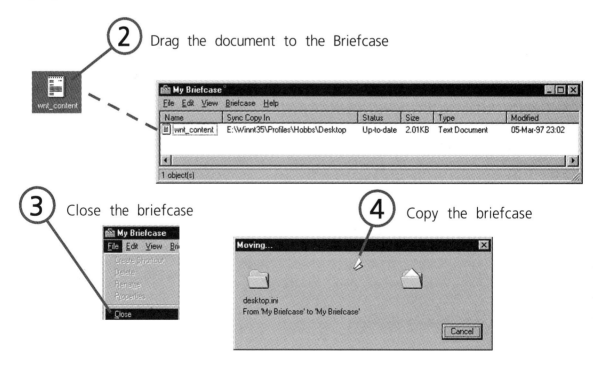

② Drag the document to the Briefcase

③ Close the briefcase

④ Copy the briefcase

Basic steps

6 Insert the floppy disk back into the main computer or connect the computer to the network.

7 Drag the Briefcase back to the Desktop.

8 Open the Briefcase.

9 Select **Briefcase**, then **Update All**.

10 Click on **Update**. The documents are now up-to-date.

④ The Briefcase has been moved to the floppy disk

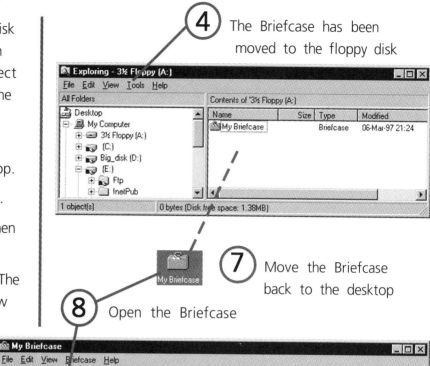

⑦ Move the Briefcase back to the desktop

⑧ Open the Briefcase

⑨ Update the Briefcase

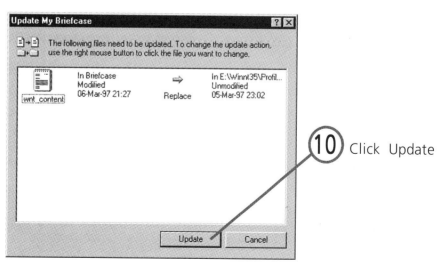

⑩ Click Update

Summary

- ❑ A **WINS** server translates computer names into IP addresses.

- ❑ A **DNS** server translates computer names into IP addresses for people using TCP/IP.

- ❑ Use the **ping** utility to check the network is working correctly.

- ❑ Use **telnet** to connect to a non-NT computer.

- ❑ Computers can be grouped into logical **workgroups**.

- ❑ Use the wizard to set up the connection to a **dial-in network**.

- ❑ Use the **dial-up monitor** to see how long you have been connected to a remote computer.

- ❑ A **modem** can be easily configured from its properties dialog box.

- ❑ Keep your files up to date using the **Briefcase**.

9 Internet

Internet or Intranet

If you haven't heard of the **Internet** then where have you been living, at the North Pole? The Internet is a worldwide network of computers. It will probably form the basis of moving us into an information age.

The Internet is proving very popular because almost everything on it is available for free.

There are a number of services available on the Internet, but the most popular ones are:

- World Wide Web
- E-mail
- Newsgroups
- FTP

Usually the information on the Internet is for everyone to use. However, companies have discovered that the Web approach is an ideal forum for publishing information exclusively for the use of its employees such as company benefits or group profiles. When a company creates an internal Web then it has created an **intranet**.

The WWW is the fastest growing part of the Internet. Not a day goes by without another company creating or updating a web site to promote the goods or services that their company provides.

Computer companies have also found that a good method for distributing updates of their software is via an FTP site, and newsgroups allow you to discuss a topic with people from around the world. There has never been a better time to start exploring the Internet.

Jargon

Internet is the global network of computers which all share information.

HTML stands for HyperText Markup Language.

World Wide Web also know as the Web or WWW. Web pages are documents written in **HTML**.

E-mail stands for Electronic mail.

Newsgroup is a place to discuss a specific subject with other Internet users.

FTP stands for File Transfer Protocol. It is a method of transferring files between computers.

Intranet is the name given to an internal web such as one within a company that contains specific company information.

Jargon

Web site is a place where people can visit and view information using a world wide web address.

FTP service will allow users to visit your computer and either copy files or put files on your computer.

Gopher is a means of creating links to other computers and helping people to find information. Recently Gopher sites have diminished since most people prefer to use the World Wide Web.

Peer Web Service consists of a web server, ftp and gopher service.

Can I join the Internet?

Windows NT provides all the necessary software to allow your computer to join the Internet. Therefore, rather than having to put your documents and files on another computer, you can configure your computer to be a **web site**.

Remember that joining the Internet or an intranet doesn't have to be limited to just providing a Web site. We have already seen that the Internet offers a wide range of services. You can configure your computer to also provide:

● **FTP** service

● **Gopher** service

Thankfully, Microsoft have made it very easy to connect your computer to the internet, by installing the **Peer Web Service**. Therefore you should be connected in a very short period of time. However, one important point to consider is that the computer must be permanently connected to the network for your Web site to be visible.

If your computer is not connected to a network then you may be asking yourself, why bother doing this? Well, if you have web pages installed with your Internet service provider, then you could test them out on your own Web site, before installing them for all the world to see.

If your computer is part of a network then creating your own Web site could be an efficient means of telling people what you are working on or answering questions. For instance, they may be able to visit your site and get the information, rather than interrupt you. So Web sites don't always have to be for fun, they do have a serious side too!

Set up a Web site

If you want to set up a simple Web site, NT Workstation provides the following three Internet services as part of Microsoft Peer Web Services:

- Web Service
- FTP Service
- Gopher Service

Everyone will want to use the Web service. The FTP service only needs to be set up if you want to share files with other users and you probably won't need to worry about the Gopher service.

1 Click the 🖧 icon in the **Control Panel**.

2 Open the **Services** tab.

3 Click the **Add** button.

4 Select **Microsoft Peer Web Services** and click **OK**.

5 Insert the NT CD into the CD-ROM drive.

6 Click **OK**.

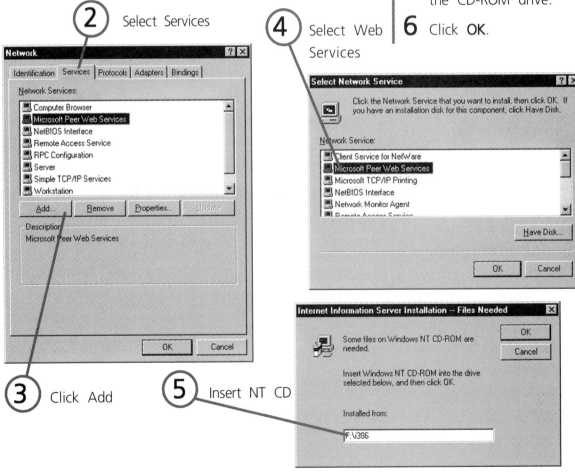

② Select Services

③ Click Add

④ Select Web Services

⑤ Insert NT CD

Basic steps

7 Select **Options** and click **OK**.

8 Optionally change the folders for the three services.

9 Files are copied.

10 Disable Guest access if FTP service is only open to authorised users.

11 Click **OK** when installation is complete.

12 Restart the computer.

⑦ Choose what to install

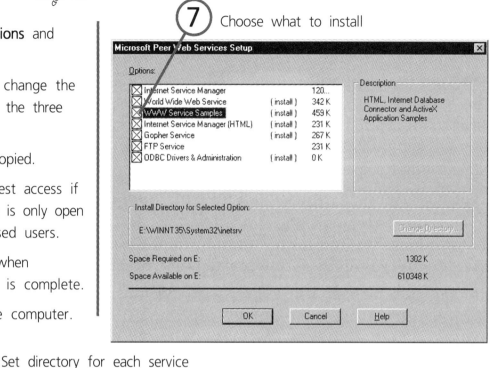

⑧ Set directory for each service

⑨ Now copying files

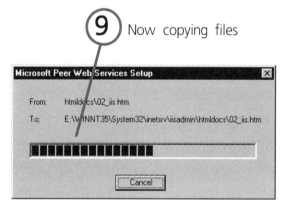

⑩ Only disable Guest access for security reasons

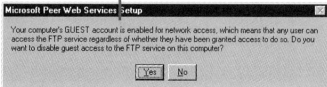

Simple HTML

Most people will install the Web services so they can turn their computer into a Web site.

Web pages are written in a language called **HTML** (Hyper Text Markup Language). Stop, before you put this book down and say oh no, not another language. This one is very easy and requires nothing more than a simple text editor like the **Notepad** in windows.

If you don't feel up to writing HTML, then there are a number of software tools which will create an **HTML document** from word processing software like Wordperfect and Microsoft Word. For more information on writing HTML refer to *Designing Internet Home Pages Made Simple*.

So what is HTML? It's a language that is written using a basic editor and is described using **tags**. A tag is an instruction contained within angle brackets. e.g. <HTML> is a tag that defines the start of a HTML document.

The golden rule to remember is that almost every tag has a partner, which begins with a forward slash that says, now finished with this tag. e.g. </HTML> defines the end of an HTML document.

HTML is very comprehensive and you can get by with only knowing a few tags. The important ones to know are:

- <TITLE>   add a title to the document
- <HEAD>   heading
- <P>   paragraph
-
               new line
- <IMG SRC= >   include an image

Jargon

HTML stands for HyperText Markup Language.

HTML Document is a text file containing HTML tags which comprise your Web page.

Notepad provided in Windows is an editing software tool. It can be found in the Accessories group.

Tags are instructions in HTML which state the action to perform, like display this text, draw a line, or use this graphic.

Tip

If ever confused how to write it in HTML, take a look at somebody else's Web page to see how they did it. Most Web browsers permit you to see the HTML used to create the Web page.

Start of
document

Title for window

Background colour

Heading

Start a paragraph

Bold text

Line break

Start a bullet list

List item

End of document

The Web page
which is displayed
from this HTML

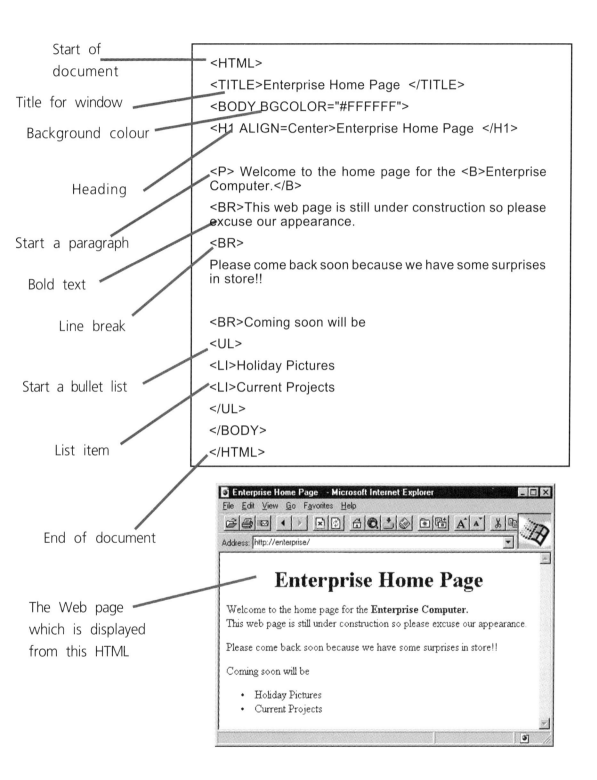

```
<HTML>
<TITLE>Enterprise Home Page  </TITLE>
<BODY BGCOLOR="#FFFFFF">
<H1 ALIGN=Center>Enterprise Home Page  </H1>

<P> Welcome to the home page for the <B>Enterprise
Computer.</B>
<BR>This web page is still under construction so please
excuse our appearance.
<BR>
Please come back soon because we have some surprises
in store!!

<BR>Coming soon will be
<UL>
<LI>Holiday Pictures
<LI>Current Projects
</UL>
</BODY>
</HTML>
```

Enterprise Home Page - Microsoft Internet Explorer

File Edit View Go Favorites Help

Address: http://enterprise/

Enterprise Home Page

Welcome to the home page for the **Enterprise Computer.**
This web page is still under construction so please excuse our appearance.

Please come back soon because we have some surprises in store!!

Coming soon will be

- Holiday Pictures
- Current Projects

Change the home page

When the Web service is first started, it is configured to display the default Web document known as the *home page*, provided by Microsoft. The first step is to change this to something more interesting and relevant to you.

This should not be considered a daunting step as we only need to write a few lines of HTML. The home page does not have to be very exciting, at least not to begin with!

1 Create an HTML document and save it in your web directory.

2 Click **Start** and select **Programs** then **Microsoft Peer Web Services** then **Internet Service Manager**

3 Double click on the **WWW** service.

4 Open the **Directories** tab.

5 Enter the name of your HTML document.

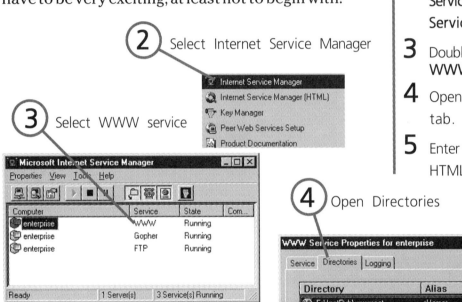

② Select Internet Service Manager

③ Select WWW service

④ Open Directories

⑥ Double click to edit Properties

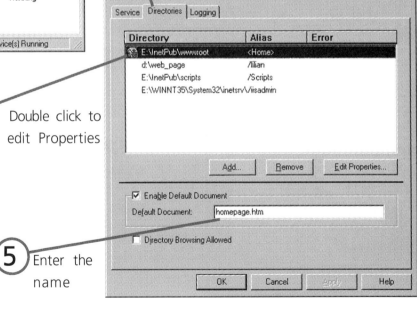

Tip

Place all web documents in their own folder.

⑤ Enter the name

128

Basic steps

6 Double click on the 🏠 icon

7 Type the name or browse for the directory where the HTML documents are stored.

8 Click **OK** to confirm.

9 Start your browser and display the home page by entering only the computer's name.

⑦ Specify the directory

Use the Browse button to locate the directory

Directory Properties

Directory: `D:\web_page`   Browse...

⦿ Ho_me Directory 🏠

○ Virtual Directory

Alias:

Account Information

User Name:

Password:

☐ Virtual Server

Virtual Server IP Address:

Access

☑ Read   ☐ Execute

☐ Require secure SSL channel (Not Installed)

OK   Cancel   Help

⑨ Enter the computer name

⑧ Click OK

View the home page

Add a Web path

When the Web service is first started, it is configured to only display HTML documents from the World Wide Web Publishing directory. Those of you familiar with surfing the Internet will know that documents are usually found using an address of the format

> http://enterprise/lilian/hobbs

So far we have only been able to retrieve a document located in the default directory. Normally documents will be placed in a number of different directories. Rather than expect the user to remember the precise location, we can setup a simple alias to point to the directory instead. e.g. the alias *lilian* points to a directory at *d:\web_page*

You can define as many aliases as you like, but it is probably a good idea to keep them to a minimum.

1 Start the **Internet Service Manager**

2 Double click on the **WWW** service.

3 Open the **Directories** tab.

4 Click **Add**.

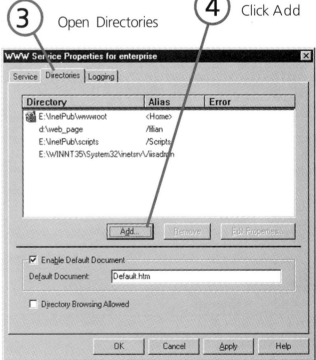

Basic steps

5 Specify the **Directory** where the HTML documents are stored.

6 Enter an **Alias** for the directory.

7 Click **OK**.

8 Using the browser display the home page by entering the computer's name, the alias and the document as a URL.

⑤ Set the directory

⑥ Type an alias

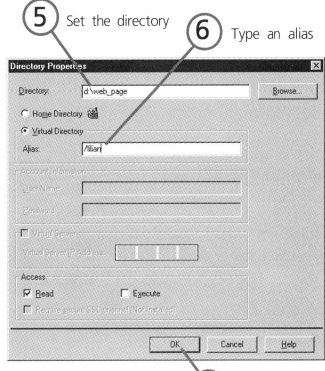

⑧ Check the alias in the browser

⑦ Click OK

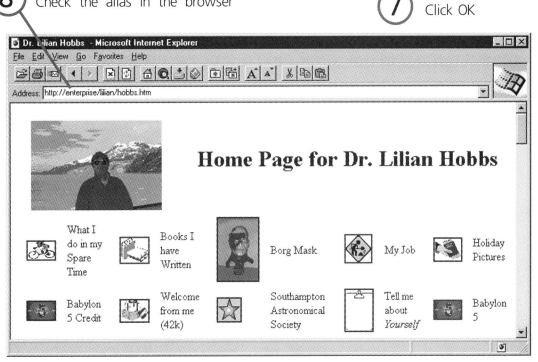

Configure the FTP service

When the services are installed, they are automatically configured and started. However, if you plan to allow FTP access to your service then there are a few customisations that you might like to perform such as:

- whether an anonymous login is allowed
- a welcome and exit message
- alias names for folders

Basic steps

1 Start the **Internet Service Manager**

2 Double click on the FTP service.

3 Open the **Services** tab.

4 Click on **Allow Anonymous Logins**.

5 Open the **Messages** tab.

6 Type your welcome message.

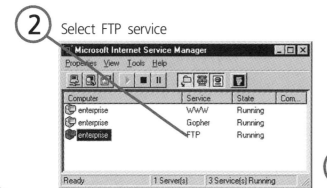

② Select FTP service

③ Open Service ④ Anonymous Logins?

⑤ Open Messages

⑥ Type your message

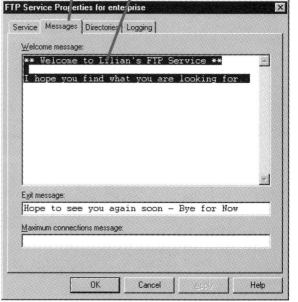

132

Basic steps

7 Open the **Directories** tab and click **Add**.

8 Select the folder.

9 Enter an Alias for the folder and click **OK**.

10 Test by clicking on **Start** then select **Run** and enter **ftp**.

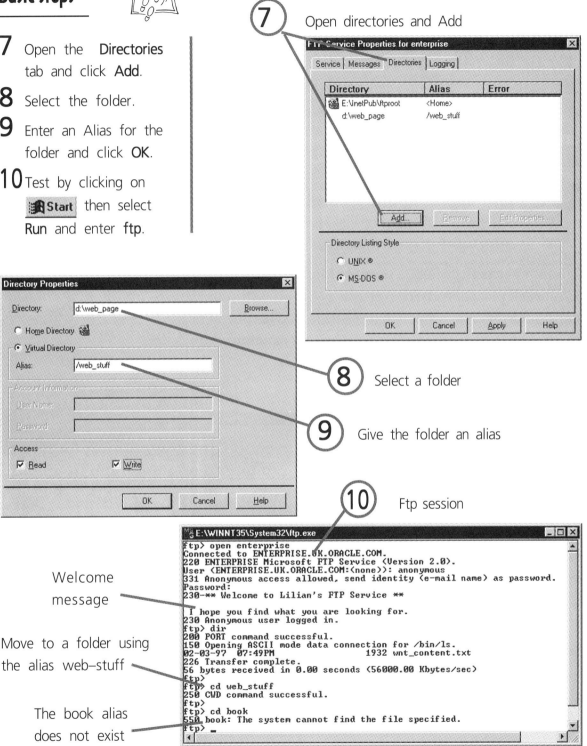

7 Open directories and Add

8 Select a folder

9 Give the folder an alias

10 Ftp session

Welcome message

Move to a folder using the alias web–stuff

The book alias does not exist

Browsers

The majority of people using the Internet will probably spend most of their time accessing the World Wide Web using a browser. There are a number of browsers available, but two of the most popular ones are:

● Microsoft Internet Explorer

● Netscape Navigator

For the latest versions of these, go to:

Internet Explorer: http://www.microsoft.com

Netscape: http://www.netscape.com

When NT was installed, a copy of Microsoft Internet Explorer is placed ready for you to use on the desktop and can be started by simply clicking on its icon. This doesn't mean that you have to use this browser, for example, the author prefers a different one.

Basic steps

1 Click on the icon on the desktop

Tip

For more on these browsers read *Netscape Made Simple* or *Internet Explorer Made Simple.*

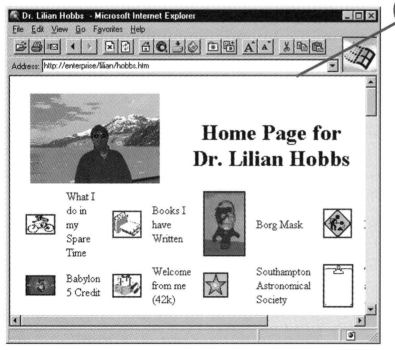

1 The author's home page

Tip

Click on the Refresh button if you suspect the page has changed since your last visit this session. Failure to do this means that you will see the old version held locally on your computer.

Jargon

URL Uniform Resource Locator.

WWW World Wide Web.

E-mail electronic mail.

Tip

Include with every e-mail message that you send, your e-mail address so that people know how to contact you.

Keep a hard copy list of the e-mail and WWW addresses you use most often. Electronic lists have a habit of falling into the Recycle Bin!

Everything on the Internet has a unique address.

World Wide Web

A document on the World Wide Web is located via its URL which is of the form:

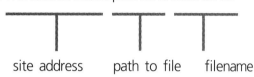

http://www.lilian.com/pub/info/latestoffer

       site address   path to file   filename

If you try to retrieve a document using an invalid address you will get an error saying that the document cannot be found.

E-mail

A typical format for e-mail addresses is

name@site.address

e.g. *lmhobbs@clara.net*

Usually an e-mail address will contain the part of the person's name in the address. Unfortunately, this is not always the case and if you send mail to a CompuServe subscriber then its quite likely that their e-mail address will be of the form 100563.777@compuserve.com. So do make sure that you have the right number or you could end up sending mail to the wrong person!

If you do send e-mail to an invalid address then you will get e-mail stating that your message could not be sent.

Using FTP

We have already seen in Chapter 7 how to connect to a computer on the network and have access to its folders and files as if they were on your own machine. Although this is a good method for copying files, it is not always the fastest and sometimes people don't want to allow you to connect to their computer. The alternative is to use a fast and efficient method for moving files around called FTP.

Windows NT supplies a simple version of FTP but you may prefer to use the shareware version shown here which is much easier to use.

To use ftp you need to know the following:

● name or internet address of the computer

● username or try anonymous

● password, if using anonymous then use your e-mail address

● file to copy and where it is stored on the computer

There are many FTP sites on the Internet and to overcome the problem of giving every user their own username and password many sites allow anonymous logins. This means that you use the username of anonymous and then supply your e-mail address as your password. Security on the host computer will ensure that you only see the files you should do, so don't expect to go exploring all the files on the host computer.

It is very important to remember to tell FTP what type of file is to be copied. Use *ascii* for text files only and *binary* for all other types of files.

Basic steps

1 Click on **Start** then select **Run** and enter ftp.

or

1 Click the **ftp** icon.

2 Specify the computer to connect to.

3 Enter your username.

4 Enter the password.

5 Specify whether **ascii** or **binary** file to copy.

6 Select the file to copy.

7 Find the local directory where the file is to be copied to.

8 Click on the arrow to specify which way to copy the file.

Tip

If you set the wrong file type, the file cannot be read.

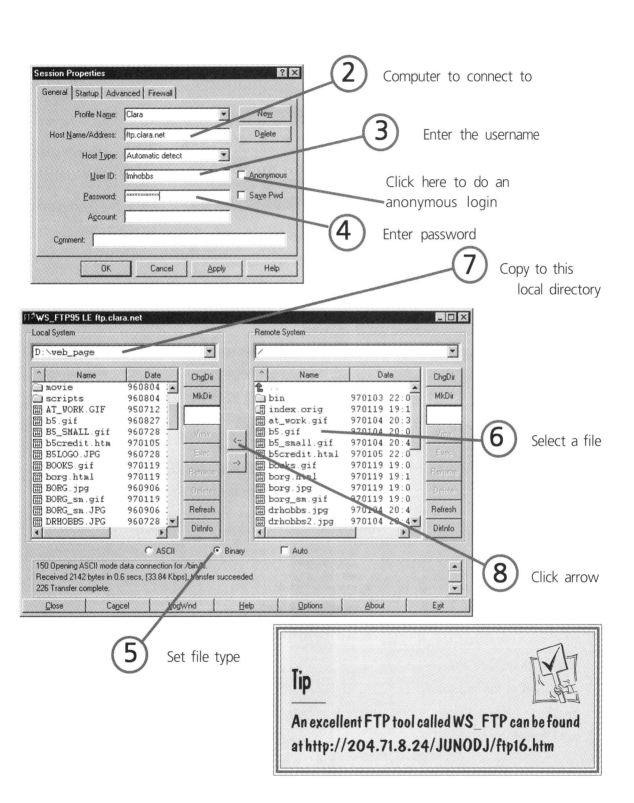

Session Properties

General | Startup | Advanced | Firewall

Profile Name: Clara

Host Name/Address: ftp.clara.net

Host Type: Automatic detect

User ID: lmhobbs ☐ Anonymous

Password: xxxxxxxxxxx ☐ Save Pwd

Account:

Comment:

OK | Cancel | Apply | Help

(2) Computer to connect to

(3) Enter the username

Click here to do an anonymous login

(4) Enter password

(7) Copy to this local directory

WS_FTP95 LE ftp.clara.net

Local System

D:\web_page

Name	Date
movie	960804
scripts	960804
AT_WORK.GIF	950712
b5.gif	960827
B5_SMALL.gif	960728
b5credit.htm	970105
B5LOGO.JPG	960728
BOOKS.gif	970119
borg.html	970119
BORG.jpg	960906
BORG_sm.gif	970119
BORG_sm.JPG	960906
DRHOBBS.JPG	960728

ChgDir | MkDir | View | Exec | Rename | Delete | Refresh | DirInfo

Remote System

/

Name	Date
..	
bin	970103 22:0
index.orig	970119 19:1
at_work.gif	970104 20:3
b5.gif	970104 20:0
b5_small.gif	970104 20:4
b5credit.html	970105 22:0
books.gif	970119 19:0
borg.html	970119 19:1
borg.jpg	970119 19:0
borg_sm.gif	970119 19:0
drhobbs.jpg	970104 20:4
drhobbs2.jpg	970104 20:4

ChgDir | MkDir | View | Exec | Rename | Delete | Refresh | DirInfo

○ ASCII ● Binary ☐ Auto

150 Opening ASCII mode data connection for /bin/ls.
Received 2142 bytes in 0.6 secs, (33.84 Kbps), transfer succeeded
226 Transfer complete.

Close | Cancel | LogWnd | Help | Options | About | Exit

(6) Select a file

(8) Click arrow

(5) Set file type

Tip

An excellent FTP tool called WS_FTP can be found at http://204.71.8.24/JUNODJ/ftp16.htm

---

Microsoft news

One of the very useful parts of the Internet that people quite often miss is the newsgroups. A newsgroup is a place where people can discuss a topic and there are over 20,000 of them on the Internet.

In a newsgroup you read an entry and then you can either ignore it, reply or start a discussion on a new thread. Since newsgroups are read by people from all over the world you can get a global view to your question. One very important point to remember is that many newsgroup are not moderated, which means that no-one is checking the quality or the relevance of the articles.

You can read any of the newsgroups, but it's usual to subscribe to a group, like subscribing to a magazine.

Unlike e-mail which is sent to you, to read the new postings in a newsgroup you must connect to the news server to retrieve the new entries.

Basic steps

1 From the **Start** menu select **Programs** then **Internet News**.

2 Click on **Newsgroups** then the **Subscribed** tab to see which groups you have subscribed to.

3 Click on **Connect**.

4 Select a newsgroup from the list.

5 Read the headers.

To subscribe to a group, select it from the All list and click Subscribe.

List all newsgroups containing the word **astro**

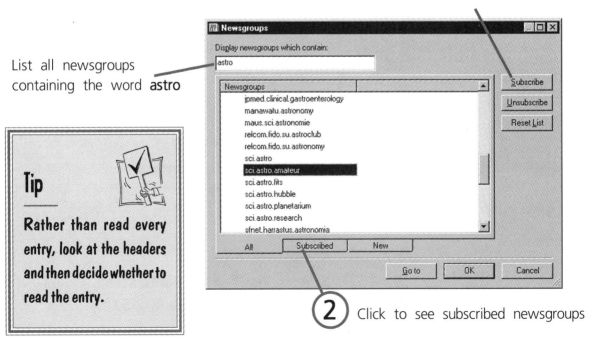

Click to see subscribed newsgroups

Tip

Rather than read every entry, look at the headers and then decide whether to read the entry.

138

Basic steps

6 Double click to read the article.

7 When you have read all the articles, click on **Edit,** then click on **Mark all as read.**

There are many different newsgroup readers available, which all behave pretty much the same. However, one very useful feature that isn't available in all newsgroup readers and can save you money if you are paying for the telephone call, is an offline reader facility. This allows you to download the headers, read them at a later time and then select which entries you want to read. You then connect again, download the articles, disconnect and then read the articles while not connected.

Software download

Microsoft news can be downloaded from:

http://www.microsoft.com/ie/imn/

④ Select a newsgroup

③ Connect

⑤ Read the headers

⑥ Read articles

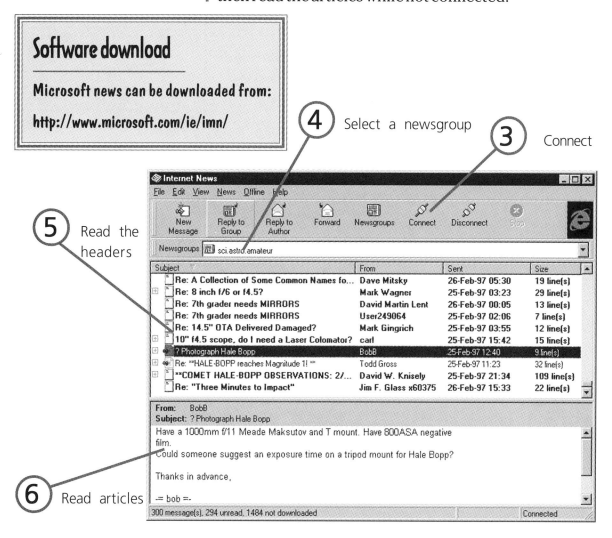

Microsoft mail

There are various ways to communicate with people, a letter, the telephone or a fax. But now there is an even better method, which is very fast and reliable, it is called electronic mail. Also known as e-mail, it's becoming very popular among people of all ages. Today you can send an e-mail message and within minutes it should arrive at its destination.

Microsoft provides Internet Mail, but as with newsgroup software, there is a wide variety of e-mail software available. Which one you choose is a matter of personal choice.

All e-mail software will ask for some setup information. If you are not sure of this information, then ask your network administrator.

1 Click **Start** and select **Programs** then **Internet Mail**.

2 Select the **Inbox** folder.

3 View the list of messages in the inbox.

4 Click on any message to read it.

5 If the message is no longer required, press the **[Delete]** key.

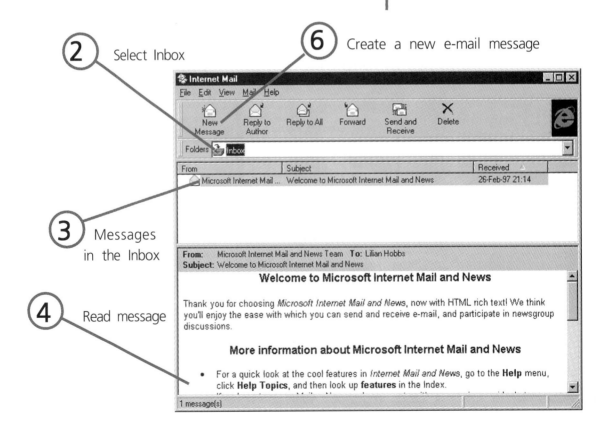

② Select Inbox

⑥ Create a new e-mail message

③ Messages in the Inbox

④ Read message

140

Basic steps

6 Click on **New Message**.

7 Enter the e-mail address of the person to receive the message.

8 Enter a **Subject** and the message.

9 Click on the **Send mail** icon.

10 Click **OK** to confirm message will be sent later.

When a message is sent to you it is usually held on the mail server. When you start your e-mail software, your messages are automatically downloaded to your Inbox.

Messages can be sent, replied to and forwarded to anyone on the Internet.

One very useful feature, is the ability to compose a mail message while not connected to your mail server. The message is then stored in your Outbox and next time you connect to the mail server, the message can be sent by clicking on the appropriate command.

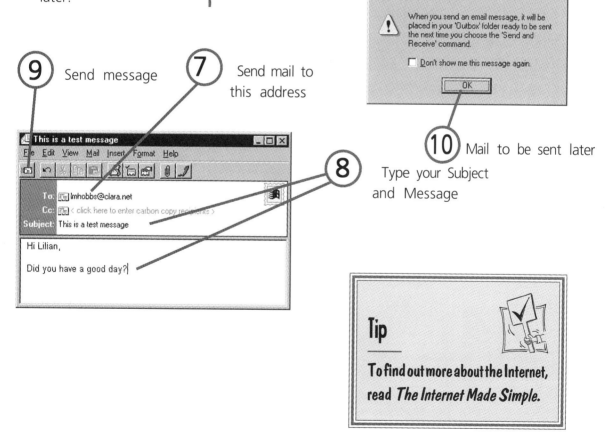

⑨ Send message

⑦ Send mail to this address

⑧

⑩ Mail to be sent later

Type your Subject and Message

Send Mail

⚠ When you send an email message, it will be placed in your 'Outbox' folder ready to be sent the next time you choose the 'Send and Receive' command.

☐ Don't show me this message again.

OK

This is a test message

File Edit View Mail Insert Format Help

To: lmhobbs@clara.net
Cc: < click here to enter carbon copy recipients >
Subject: This is a test message

Hi Lilian,

Did you have a good day?|

Tip

To find out more about the Internet, read *The Internet Made Simple*.

Summary

- ❑ The **Internet** is a global network of computers.

- ❑ The **intranet** is an web-like network operating within one organisation.

- ❑ Windows NT comes ready to provide **World Wide Web, FTP** and **Gopher services.**

- ❑ Install **Microsoft Peer Web Services** to provide Internet services on your computer.

- ❑ Web documents are written in **HTML**.

- ❑ Use **Internet Service Manager** to configure the Web default page and access to directories.

- ❑ The FTP service can be configured to allow **anonymous access.**

- ❑ Windows NT automatically installs the **browser** Microsoft Internet Explorer.

- ❑ Use **FTP** to move files between computers.

- ❑ Internet newsgroups can be read using **Internet News.**

- ❑ Electronic mail can be sent using **Internet Mail.**

Glossary

Access rights

Determine the actions that a user or group of users can perform such as access the computer from the network, load and unload device drivers.

Auditing

NT logs certain events into a file.

Briefcase

A facility provided in NT for removing files from the computer and taking them to another computer. When the files are returned to the original computer, the Briefcase will ensure that all copies of the file are the latest.

Browser

The application program which displays World Wide Web pages.

Computer name

The unique name given to the computer. It can be no longer than 15 characters.

Control panel

This window contains all the applications that are used to configure the computer.

Default printer

The printer used by all applications when they are asked to print a file.

Disk Administrator

The application which is used to manage disks, performing such tasks as formatting a new disk.

Disk signature

Written to a disk by the Disk Administrator so that it can be accessed by this tool.

Domain Name Service (DNS)

A service for translating computer names into IP addresses. Computers on the network will be deemed as DNS servers and their IP addresses are available from your network administrator.

Emergency Repair Disk

A floppy disk which contains the NT configuration for a computer. It must be kept safe and updated whenever the hardware configuration changes.

Event Viewer

An application which allows you to see the contents of the security and application log and to define what information must be collected in the log.

File Allocation Table (FAT)

The file system used by DOS. A disk formatted as FAT can be accessed by computers running Windows 95 or Windows for Workgroups.

Folders

Sub-divisions created on the disk to hold files and applications. They are very similar to the directories used by other operating systems.

Group

A name given to a collection of users which specifies what this user may do. Group names are managed in the User Manager application.

Hardware profile

A configuration saved by NT which refers to a specific set of hardware available on the computer, e.g. a configuration with a tape drive

Host file

A file used to translate computer names to a TCP/IP address.

Internet

The Internet is a world wide network of computers that all share information.

Intranet

An intranet is the same as the Internet except that the computers are all located on an internal private network such as within a company.

IP address

An address of the format aa.bb.cc.dd which uniqely identifies every computer on a TCP/IP network.

Local area network (LAN)

A set of computers connected by a cable. Typically they are all in the same building.

Logon

The process of connecting to a computer by specifying a username and password.

Mapping a network drive

Connecting to a shared disk on a remote computer as if it were a local drive.

Multi-tasking

The ability to execute multiple jobs at the same time.

Multi-threading

An application which can execute multiple tasks at the same time.

NetBEUI

A network transport used by Microsoft networking.

Network protocol

Is a defined way of communicating with other computers. Examples of network protocols are TCP/IP and NETBEUI.

NT Workstation

A version of the Microsoft NT operating system that offers almost, but not all of the features of the NT Server version.

NTFS

The NT file system which offers additional security over the FAT system. NTFS disks cannot be read by computers running Windows for Workgroups or Windows 95.

Partition

A means of dividing a single disk into a number of smaller disks. Every disk must have at least one partition.

PING

A very useful application for testing that a TCP/IP network is working correctly.

Print queue

The place where all documents are held until they are printed.

Recycle Bin

The place where deleted files are located, allowing them to be recovered in the event of accidental erase. A file is not actually deleted until the Recycle Bin is emptied.

Registry

The place in NT where all the configuration information for the computer is held.

Service

A software routine that performs a specific function. They are many of them in NT. They belong to the NT operating system and application software such as database or World Wide Web services.

Sharing

The process of allowing a resource such as a disk or printer to be accessed by users on other computers.

Shortcut

A quick means of retrieving a document or activating an application by clicking on the icon which represents it.

Start button

Found on the Taskbar, the place where applications are launched from.

Taskbar

The place on the Desktop where you can see all the applications that are running, and start new applications and retrieve documents from the Start button.

TCP/IP

Stands for Transport Control Protocol/Internet Protocol and is a very popular network protocol.

Username

A unique name required by every user who logons to the computer.

Virtual memory

Space on the hard disk that is reserved by NT to emulate memory.

Windows Internet Naming Service (WINS)

Another service for translating names into IP addresses. Also see *DNS*.

Workgroup

A name given to a collection of computers. It is a useful concept in NT for grouping computers together.

Index